Contents

S0-BDO-371

Problem Solving Strategies 4, SV 0515-4

Introduction

The National Council of Teachers of Mathematics (NCTM) has set specific standards to help students become confident of their mathematical abilities. Communicating mathematically and problem solving are the keys to helping students develop skills to apply in their daily lives and in later careers.

Based on the belief that students learn to reason mathematically in order to become problem solvers, the strategies in this book show students more than one way to solve problems. These strategies are not absolute techniques, however. Learning a multitude of ways to approach a problem is part of the philosophy in developing sets of problem solving strategies.

Organization

The first chapter, Working with Numbers, is a review for students at this level who may need additional practice. The other nine chapters offer several strategies to solve a given type of problem: Addition, Subtraction, Multiplication, Division, Mixed Operations, Fractions, Decimals and Money, Measurement, and Logic. Each lesson begins with an introductory problem which is solved using a series of clearly defined steps. The practice problems are based on real-life situations and demonstrate use of this set of steps to reach a solution.

Special Feature

Each chapter concludes with a "Flex Your Math Muscles" activity page that presents an opportunity for students to choose their own strategy to solve problems. These pages provide students with a unique way to approach the challenges. Divergent thinking is promoted in these lessons.

Problem Solving Strategies

The following problem solving strategies are demonstrated:

CHOOSE AN OPERATION   Students determine which operation (addition, subtraction, multiplication, or division) to use based on the information presented.

USE ESTIMATION   Students learn both when and how to estimate answers, based on rounding numbers and performing the appropriate operation. Estimation is encouraged as a strategy in all problem solving to verify reasonableness of answers.

FIND A PATTERN   This strategy emphasizes pattern recognition of given sequences of numbers, geometric shapes, pictorial information, and other data for problem solving.

GUESS AND CHECK   Students learn a variety of methods to reduce the number of trial and error efforts needed to reach accuracy in answers.

IDENTIFY EXTRA OR MISSING INFORMATION   By identifying pertinent information, students learn to recognize information which is extra or missing.

MAKE A DRAWING   Creating visual images of information makes analysis of the facts easier.

MAKE A LIST   Students learn to organize information into meaningful lists for later matching or computation.

MAKE A TABLE   Pattern recognition, identification of extra or missing information, and arrangement of data into a visual form demonstrate the effectiveness of making a table.

USE A GRAPH   Graphing organizes information so that comparisons can be made visually.

IDENTIFY SUBSTEPS   Some complex problems require the completion of more than one step to calculate the solution. This strategy emphasizes the importance of identifying both the given information and the order of operations to reach the solution.

USE LOGICAL REASONING   In this strategy students learn to recognize relationships and to answer the question, "Does it make sense?" Strategies include a process of elimination of answers and visual representation of information to organize the elements of a problem.

WORK BACKWARD This section introduces a strategy for solving complex problems in which the end result is given. By recognizing clue words and using them to solve the problem, students can work backward from an answer. This skill develops background for later success in algebra.

WRITE A NUMBER SENTENCE Converting written statements into numerical sentences to solve for an unknown is the basis of an algebraic approach. This strategy demonstrates identification of known and unknown information to develop sentences for solutions.

Use

This book is designed for independent use by students who have had instruction in the specific skills covered in these lessons. Copies of the activities can be given to individuals, pairs of students, or small groups for completion. They can also be used as a center activity. If students are familiar with the content, the worksheets can be homework for reviewing and reinforcing problem solving concepts.

To begin, determine the implementation that fits your students' needs and your classroom structure. The following plan suggests a format for this implementation:

1. *Explain* the purpose of the worksheets to your class.
2. *Review* the mechanics of how you want students to work with the exercises.
3. *Review* the specific skill for the students who may not remember the process for successful completion of the computation.
4. *Introduce* students to the process and to the purpose of the activities.
5. *Do* a practice activity together.
6. *Allow* students to experiment, discover, and explore a variety of ways to solve a given problem.

Additional Notes

1. *Bulletin Board.* Display completed worksheets to show student progress.
2. *Center Activities.* Use the worksheets as center activities to give students the opportunity to work cooperatively.

3. *Have fun.* Working with these activities can be fun as well as meaningful for you and your students.

What Research Says

The National Council of Teachers of Mathematics (NCTM) has listed problem solving as a key standard for instructional programs for all students. According to NCTM,

Problem solving is the cornerstone of school mathematics. Without the ability to solve problems, the usefulness and power of mathematical ideas, knowledge, and skills are severely limited. Students who can efficiently and accurately multiply but who cannot identify situations that call for multiplication are not well prepared. Students who can both develop *and* carry out a plan to solve a mathematical problem are exhibiting knowledge that is much deeper and more useful than simply carrying out a computation. Unless students can solve problems, the facts, concepts, and procedures they know are of little use. The goal of school mathematics should be for all students to become increasingly able and willing to engage with and solve problems.

Problem solving is also important because it can serve as a vehicle for learning new mathematical ideas and skills (Schroeder and Lester 1989). A problem-centered approach to teaching mathematics uses interesting and well-selected problems to launch mathematical lessons and engage students. In this way, new ideas, techniques, and mathematical relationships emerge and become the focus of discussion. Good problems can inspire the exploration of important mathematical ideas, nurture persistence, and reinforce the need to understand and use various strategies, mathematical properties, and relationships.

National Council of Teachers of Mathematics. *Principles and Standards for School Mathematics.* Reston, Va.: The National Council of Teachers of Mathematics, 2000.

Schroeder, Thomas L., and Frank K. Lester, Jr. "Developing Understanding in Mathematics via Problem Solving." In *New Directions for Elementary School Mathematics,* 1989 Yearbook of the National Council of Teachers of Mathematics, edited by Paul R. Trafton, pp. 31–42. Reston, Va.: National Council of Teachers of Mathematics, 1989.

Correlation to NCTM Standards

Content Strands	Pages
Number and Operations	
Understand the place-value structure of the base-ten number system and be able to represent and compare whole numbers and decimals	10, 11, 12, 13, 16, 17, 18, 19
Develop fluency with basic number combinations for multiplication and division and use these combinations to mentally compute problems	53
Develop fluency in adding, subtracting, multiplying, and dividing	14, 15, 16, 22, 23, 24, 25, 26, 27, 28, 29, 31, 32, 33, 35, 36, 37, 38, 39, 40, 41, 44, 45, 46, 47, 48, 49, 50, 51, 52, 56, 57, 58, 59, 60, 61, 62, 63, 65, 66, 67, 68, 69, 86
Develop and use strategies to estimate computations involving decimals in situations relevant to students' experience	80, 81, 82, 83, 84, 85, 87, 88, 89
Use visual models, benchmarks, and equivalent forms to add and subtract decimals	80, 81, 82
Develop understanding of fractions as parts of unit wholes	70, 71
Develop and use strategies to estimate computations involving fractions	73, 74, 75, 76, 77, 78, 79
Use visual models, benchmarks, and equivalent forms to add and subtract commonly used fractions	72
Algebra	
Describe, extend, and make generalizations about geometric and numeric patterns	14, 17, 44, 47, 52, 57

Correlation Chart, page 2

Content Strands	Pages
Measurement	
Understand the need for measuring with standard units and become familiar with standard units in the customary and metric systems	90, 91, 92, 95, 96, 97, 98, 99
Carry out simple unit conversions, such as from centimeters to meters, within a system of measurement	93
Select and use benchmarks to estimate measurements	94
Data Analysis and Probability	
Represent data using tables and graphs such as line plots, bar graphs, and line graphs	12, 13, 18, 19, 20, 21, 30, 34, 37, 38, 42, 43, 48, 54, 55, 64, 68, 100, 101, 102, 103, 104, 106, 107
Predict the probability of outcomes of simple experiments and test the predictions	103, 104, 105, 106, 107, 108
Problem Solving	
Build new mathematical knowledge through problem solving	all
Solve problems that arise in mathematics and in other contexts	all
Apply and adapt a variety of appropriate strategies to solve problems	all
Monitor and reflect on the process of mathematical problem solving	all

Name _____ Date _____

Assessment, page 1

Follow the directions to solve each problem.

For questions 1–2, find a pattern to solve the problem. Write the number that comes next in each pattern.

1. 335, 340, 345, 350, _____

299, 399, 499, 599, _____

45, 54, 63, 72, _____

2. 800, 750, 700, 650, _____

125, 150, 175, 200, _____

14, 21, 28, 35, _____

For questions 3–4, make a table of the facts to solve the problem.

Mick's Marvelous Movie Theater was showing a cartoon and an adventure movie last weekend. On Friday 15 tickets were sold for the cartoon, and 13 tickets were sold for the adventure. On Saturday 20 tickets were sold for the cartoon, and 21 tickets were sold for the adventure movie. On Sunday 15 tickets were sold for the cartoon, and 12 tickets were sold for the adventure.

3. On which day were the most tickets sold for the adventure?

_____

4. What was the total number of tickets sold for both movies on Friday?

_____

Problem Solving Strategies 4, SV 0515-4

Assessment, page 2

For questions 5–6, find and draw a line through the extra information in the problem. Then solve the problem.

5. Joy plays basketball for the Panthers. On Monday Joy scored 27 points. On Friday she scored 15 points. Joy's best friend scored 13 points on Friday. How many total points did Joy score in the two days?

_____

6. The pet store has 8 puppies and 7 kittens. It also has 9 sizes of dog and cat collars. How many puppies and kittens are at the store?

_____

For questions 7–8, round to the nearest hundred, then estimate to solve the problem.

7. There were 2,349 people watching the parade. Then it started to rain, so 542 people went home. About how many people stayed to watch the parade?

_____

8. There are 1,115 students at Lincoln School. Lee School has 984 students. About how many more students attend Lincoln than Lee?

_____

For questions 9–10, work backward to solve each problem.

9. The pet shop sold 70 guppies last weekend. There were 532 guppies left. How many guppies did the pet shop have before the weekend?

_____

10. On Wednesday Aiko counted 132 goldfish in her tank. Tuesday she had added 47 fish to the tank. How many fish did she have before Tuesday?

_____

Assessment, page 3

For questions 11–14, choose an operation, then solve the problem.

11. Many softball games were played at the picnic. There were 72 players. If each team has 9 members, how many teams were at the picnic? Circle the correct operation.

$$
\begin{array}{r}
72 \\
\times\ \ 9 \\
\hline
??
\end{array}
\qquad
72 \div 9 = ?
$$

_____

12. There are 16 picnic tables at the park. Each table seats 8 people. How many people can sit at picnic tables? Circle the correct operation.

$$
\begin{array}{r}
16 \\
\times\ \ 8 \\
\hline
??
\end{array}
\qquad
16 \div 8 = ?
$$

_____

13. Wilson counted a total of 144 cars that he passed on his way to his grandmother's house. It took 12 hours to get there. How many cars did Wilson pass each hour?

_____

14. A miner found $2\frac{3}{8}$ ounces of gold. He used $1\frac{1}{8}$ ounces to buy some supplies. How much gold did he have left?

_____

For questions 15–16, use guess and check to solve each problem.

15. Toby's bag of apples weighs 8 pounds more than his bag of oranges. The two bags weigh 24 pounds total. How much does the bag of apples weigh?

_____

16. Toby and Travis are brothers. Toby is 3 years older than Travis. The sum of their ages is 37. How old is Toby?

_____

Name _____ Date _____

Assessment, page 4

For questions 17–20, use more than one step to solve each problem.

17. At the Party Shop, Liz bought 7 balloons at 28 cents each and 4 whistles at 33 cents each. She gave the clerk a $5.00 bill. How much change did she get?

_____

18. Jack bought 2 piñatas for a party. He gave the sales clerk $35.00 and received $3.80 change. How much did each piñata cost?

_____

19. Nick, the elephant keeper, had 8 bushels of apples. There were 38 apples in a bushel. Nick gave 4 bushels of apples to Sue, who made taffy apples. How many apples were left to feed the elephant?

_____

20. Sam works 5 hours doing chores. His dad pays him $4 an hour. Then Sam buys a baseball glove for $13 and a comic book for $1.19. How much money does Sam have left?

_____

For questions 21–22, write two <u>units</u> of measurement for each item.

21. A flagpole:

weight:_____   height:_____

22. A swimming pool:

length:_____   capacity:_____

For questions 23–24, use logic to solve each problem.

23. Warren, Ilda, and John each ate a piece of pizza. One pizza is sausage, one is cheese, and one is mushroom. Warren had meat on his pizza. John is allergic to mushrooms. Who will eat the mushroom pizza?

_____

24. Blake, Alex, and Logan each hold a different color card in a card game. One card is blue, one is green, and one is red. Blake does not have a red card. Logan has the green card. Who has the red card?

_____

Assessment
Problem Solving Strategies 4, SV 0515-4

PUTTING THINGS IN THEIR PLACES

Strategy: Understand Place Value

Every 2-digit number has a tens place and a ones place.

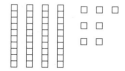

Tens	Ones
4	7	= 47

Every 3-digit number has a hundreds place, a tens place, and a ones place.

Count the groups of hundreds, tens, and ones.

Hundreds	Tens	Ones
1	6	3	= 163

Every 4-digit number has a thousands place, a hundreds place, a tens place, and a ones place.

Count the groups of thousands, hundreds, tens, and ones.

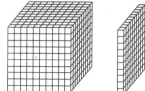 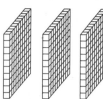

TH	H	T	O
1	3	4	2	= 1,342

Unit 1, Working with Numbers
Problem Solving Strategies 4, SV 0515-4

EVERYTHING IN ITS PLACE

Strategy: Understand Place Value

Try It! Count the groups of tens and ones. Then write the numerals.

Tens	Ones
4	8

= 48

1.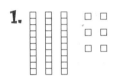

Tens	Ones

= _____

Count the groups of hundreds, tens, and ones. Then write the numerals.

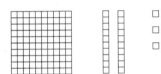

Hundreds	Tens	Ones
1	2	7

= 127

2.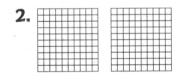

Hundreds	Tens	Ones

= _____

Count the groups of thousands, hundreds, tens, and ones. Then write the numerals.

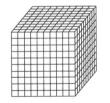 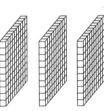

TH	H	T	O
1	3	4	2

= 1,342

3.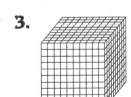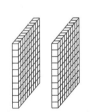

TH	H	T	O

= _____

Unit 1, Working with Numbers
Problem Solving Strategies 4, SV 0515-4

LINING THINGS UP

Strategy: Make a Table

When adding numbers, start with the digits in the ones place. It helps to make a table.

Find 214 + 465.

Add the ones.

H	T	O
2	1	4
+ 4	6	5
		9

Add the tens.

H	T	O
2	1	4
+ 4	6	5
	7	9

Add the hundreds.

H	T	O
2	1	4
+ 4	6	5
6	7	9

Try It!   Make a table. Line up the numbers, then add.

1.

T	O
2	5
+	4
2	9

T	O
4	6
+	3

	5	3
+	4	2

	3	4
+	5	5

	1	7
+	5	4	2

	5	1	7
+	1	6	2

Sometimes you have to regroup. Start with the digits in the ones place and regroup as needed.

Find 974 + 346.

Add the ones.
Regroup.

H	T	O
	1	
9	7	4
+ 3	4	6
		0

Add the tens.
Regroup.

H	T	O
	1	1
9	7	4
+ 3	4	6
	2	0

Add the hundreds.
Regroup.

TH	H	T	O
	1	1	1
	9	7	4
+	3	4	6
1	3	2	0

Try It!   Make a table. Line up the numbers, then add. Regroup as needed.

2.

T	O
3	6
+ 4	5
8	1

T	O
2	9
+ 3	2

	8	5	3
+		3	9

	3	6
+ 3	8	2

	8	2	7
+ 4	9	6

	4	7	5
+ 7	1	5

WHAT'S THE NUMBER?

Strategy: Use a Table

A place-value table can help you understand whole numbers. Each digit in a number has a value based on its place in the number.

The 3 is in the millions place.
Its value is 3 millions, or 3,000,000.

The 8 is in the hundred thousands place.
Its value is 8 hundred thousands, or 800,000.

The 6 is in the tens place.
Its value is 6 tens, or 60.

Hundred Millions	Ten Millions	Millions	Hundred Thousands	Ten Thousands	Thousands	Hundreds	Tens	Ones
		3	8	0	2	5	6	7

Try It! Write each number in the place value table.

1. 409
2. 61,023
3. 8,921,800
4. 647,369

	Hundred Millions	Ten Millions	Millions	Hundred Thousands	Ten Thousands	Thousands	Hundreds	Tens	Ones
1.							4	0	9
2.									
3.									
4.									

Write each number in the table. Then write the place name for the 2 in each number.

5. 361,250   _____hundreds_____
6. 2,035   _____
7. 592   _____
8. 24,837   _____

5.								
6.								
7.								
8.								

Write each number in the table. Then write the value of the underlined digit.

9. 6<u>3</u>,429   _____3 thousands_____
10. 17,60<u>1</u>   _____
11. 5<u>8</u>4   _____
12. 4<u>0</u>9,576   _____

9.								
10.								
11.								
12.								

PATTERNS ARE EVERYWHERE

Strategy: Find a Pattern

Patterns are how things are ordered. You can solve some problems by looking for a pattern.

STEP 1 ▷ **Read the problem.**

The picture shows the necklace Lashad is making. Lashad is using a pattern to make the necklace. How will the necklace look when she adds 3 more beads?

STEP 2 ▷ **Find the pattern and write the rule.**

2 small dotted beads and 1 large striped bead.

STEP 3 ▷ **Solve the problem.**

This is how the necklace will look after Lashad adds 3 more beads.

Try It!   Find the pattern to solve the problems.

1. A new store has flags outside. Draw the shapes of the next 3 flags in the row.

2. Write the missing number: 12, 22, 32, 42, _____, 62

3. Draw the item that goes next in the pattern.

4. Write the next two numbers: 117, 119, 121, _____, _____

NUMBERS AND WORDS

Stragegy: Write Numbers in Words and Digits

Write each number in words.

1. An airplane can fly at 32,000 feet over sea level.

Thirty-two thousand

2. Pikes Peak, a mountain in Colorado, is 14,110 feet above sea level.

_____

_____

3. Denver, Colorado, is called the "Mile-high" City because it is 1 mile above sea level. There are 5,280 feet in a mile.

_____

_____

4. There are 86,400 seconds in a day.

_____

_____

5. The ostrich is the largest bird. It can weigh up to 344 pounds.

_____

_____

6. The Statue of Liberty is 302 feet high.

_____

_____

Write each number in digits.

7. The largest cloud, called cumulonimbus, can weigh up to one billion pounds.

_____

8. The Egyptian Sphinx is two hundred forty feet long.

_____

9. Jupiter measures almost eighty-nine thousand miles across.

_____

Write each number in digits and in words.

10. The number of people in your school:

_____

_____

11. The number of people in your class:

_____

_____

Name _____ Date _____

WHAT'S THAT NUMBER?

Strategy: Write Numbers in Words and Digits

We read and write the number in the place-value chart as twenty-five thousand, three hundred seventy.

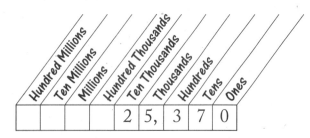

The digit 2 means 2 ten thousands, or 20,000.

The digit 5 means 5 thousands, or 5,000.

The digit 3 means 3 hundreds, or 300.

The digit 7 means 7 tens, or 70.

The digit 0 means 0 ones, or 0.

Notice that commas separate the digits into groups of three. This helps make larger numbers easier to read.

Try It! Rewrite each number. Insert commas where needed.

1. 289701 _289,701_   156823 _____   16208329 _____

2.   8067 _____   76170 _____   741038 _____

3. 9265081 _____   1972493 _____   928492 _____

Try It! Write each number in digits. Insert commas where needed.

4. Four hundred sixty thousand, nine hundred twelve   _460,912_

5. Three million, eighty-one thousand, fifty-six   _____

6. Seventy thousand, one hundred thirty-nine   _____

Name _____ Date _____

Unit 1 Review

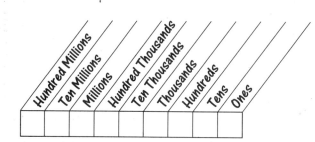

Show What You Know!

Solve each problem. Identify the strategy you used.

1. What is the place name for the 7 in 271,038?

_____

2. Make a table. Line up the numbers. Then add.

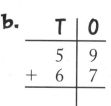

a.

T	O
1	4
+ 3	2

b.

T	O
5	9
+ 6	7

_____

3. Write the number in words. The population of Smithtown is 4,139.

_____

_____

4. Write the next 2 numbers. 29, 32, 35, _____, _____

_____

5. Count the groups of thousands, hundreds, tens, and ones. Then write the numerals in the table.

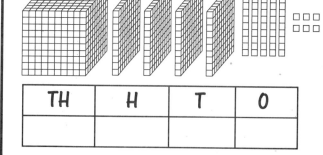

TH	H	T	O

_____

6. Write the number in digits. two hundred nine thousand, fifty-three

_____

_____

Unit 1 Review, page 2

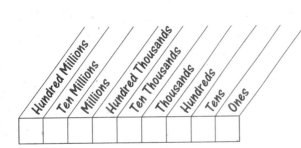

```
Hundred Millions | Ten Millions | Millions | Hundred Thousands | Ten Thousands | Thousands | Hundreds | Tens | Ones
```

Strategies

- Understand Place Value
- Make a Table
- Use a Table
- Find a Pattern
- Write Numbers in Words and Digits

Show What You Know!

Solve each problem. Identify the strategy you used.

1. Write each of the following numbers in the place-value table.

 a. 940,331,572

 b. 102,385

 c. 1,096

	Hundred Millions	Ten Millions	Millions	Hundred Thousands	Ten Thousands	Thousands	Hundreds	Tens	Ones
a.									
b.									
c.									

_____

2. Make a table. Line up the numbers. Then add.

a.

H	T	O
5	1	9
+	8	7

b.

TH	H	T	O
	8	3	6
+	7	9	2

_____

3. What is the place name for the 7 in 8,107?

_____

4. Count the groups of thousands, hundreds, tens, and ones. Then write the numerals in the table.

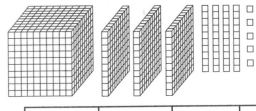

TH	H	T	O

_____

5. Draw the next two shapes in the pattern.

△ □ ○ △ △ □ ○ △ □ ___ ___

Name _____ Date _____

FLEX YOUR MATH MUSCLES

1

Flex Mathews isn't very handy with place value. Every number is out of place, it seems to him. He is trying to build a place-value chart for the number seven thousand, three hundred two, but something is wrong. Make a new place-value chart to help Flex.

Hundred Millions	Ten Millions	Millions	Hundred Thousands	Ten Thousands	Thousands	Hundreds	Tens	Ones
					7	3	2	0

2

Flex can't figure out why this problem is wrong. You can switch two numbers in the ones place to correct this problem. Which numbers can you switch? Help Flex correct this problem.

$412 - 251 = 163$

_____

3

You have a number with 3 thousands, 9 hundreds, 5 tens, and 4 ones. Make a place-value chart and write the number. What place value changes if you take away 300? _____

Write the new number in the chart below the old number.

Hundred Millions	Ten Millions	Millions	Hundred Thousands	Ten Thousands	Thousands	Hundreds	Tens	Ones

4

Flex still can't catch on to place value. He wrote nine hundreds, three thousands, seven ones, and five tens. What is wrong with this number? Write, in digits, the number you think Flex meant to write. Then correctly write the number in words.

_____

_____

Name _____ Date _____

MAMMA MIA!
THAT'S A LOT OF PIZZAS!

Strategy: Make a Table

Sometimes a problem has many facts. Putting the facts in a table can help you see how the facts go together. Then the problem is easier to solve.

STEP 1 **Read the problem.**

Jack works in Pete's Peppy Pizza Parlor on weekends when they sell the most pizzas. On Saturday he sold 40 cheese pizzas, 32 sausage pizzas, and 55 pepperoni pizzas. On Sunday he sold 12 cheese pizzas, 24 sausage pizzas, and 37 pepperoni pizzas. A cheese pizza costs $2.00, a sausage pizza costs $4.00, and a pepperoni pizza costs $5.00. Which kind of pizza did Jack sell the most this weekend?

STEP 2 **List the facts.**

Fact 1: *On Saturday Jack sold 40 cheese pizzas, 32 sausage pizzas, and 55 pepperoni pizzas. On Sunday Jack sold 12 cheese pizzas, 24 sausage pizzas, and 37 pepperoni pizzas.*

Fact 2: *A cheese pizza costs $2.00, a sausage pizza costs $4.00, and a pepperoni pizza costs $5.00*

STEP 3 **Make a table.**

Put all the facts into the table.

STEP 4 **Add. Solve the problem.**

Add the number of each kind of pizza.

$$\begin{array}{r} 40 \\ + 12 \\ \hline 52 \end{array} \text{cheese} \qquad \begin{array}{r} 32 \\ + 24 \\ \hline 56 \end{array} \text{sausage} \qquad \begin{array}{r} 55 \\ + 37 \\ \hline 92 \end{array} \text{pepperoni}$$

Jack sold pepperoni pizzas the most.

MAMMA MIA! LOTS MORE PIZZAS!

Strategy: Make a Table

	Cheese Pizza $2.00	Sausage Pizza $4.00	Pepperoni Pizza $5.00
Saturday	40	32	55
Sunday	12	24	37
Totals			

Try It! Fill in the table, then solve the problems.

1. How many sausage pizzas did Jack sell on both days?

_____

2. On which day did Jack sell the most pizzas?

_____

3. Which pizza costs the most?

_____

4. How much would it cost to buy one of each kind of pizza?

_____

5. How many and what kinds of pizzas could you buy that total exactly $9.00? (HINT: there are two correct answers.)

_____

_____

6. You want to buy 2 cheese pizzas and 3 pepperoni pizzas for a party. How much will they cost?

_____

Name _____   Date _____

SHEILA SELLS SEASHELLS BY THE SEASHORE!

Strategy: Identify Extra Information

Some problems may give more facts than you need. Read the problem. Decide which facts you need and which are extra. Cross out the extra facts. Use the facts that are left to solve the problem.

STEP 1 **Read the problem.**
Sheila collects seashells at the beach. She sells them for $1.00 each. One week she found 34 shells. The next week she found 16 shells. How many shells did Sheila find during those 2 weeks?

STEP 2 **Decide which facts you need.**
Fact 1: *The first week she found 34 shells.*
Fact 2: *The next week she found 16 shells.*

STEP 3 **Decide which facts are extra.**
She sells them for $1.00 each.

STEP 4 **Add. Solve the problem.**
34 + 16 = 50
Sheila found 50 shells in 2 weeks.

Try It! Cross out extra facts. Then solve the problems.

1. 14 girls and 18 boys went swimming. Each girl wore a red bathing suit. How many children went swimming?

_____

2. Pedro plays beach volleyball. His team plays 20 games during a season. So far they have won 6 games and lost 3. How many games has the team played this season?

_____

Unit 2, Addition
Problem Solving Strategies 4, SV 0515-4

Name _____ Date _____

HOW MANY?
ABOUT THAT MANY!

Strategy: Use Estimation

You do not always need an exact answer to solve a problem. You can solve such problems by estimating. To estimate, round each number to the same place. Then add the rounded numbers.

STEP 1 **Read the problem.**
About how much is 64 + 37? (Remember, *about* means you do not need an exact answer.)

STEP 2 **Round each number to the nearest tens place.**
64 → 60   37 → 40

STEP 3 **Add. Solve the problem.**
60 + 40 = 100

Try It! Round the numbers to the nearest tens place, then add.

1. Miss Garcia's class held a bake sale. They sold 66 cupcakes and 53 cookies. About how many cupcakes and cookies did they sell altogether?

66 → _____   53 → _____

_____

2. 122 fathers and 96 mothers went to the school's open house. About how many parents went to the open house?

122 → _____   96 → _____

_____

3. The cafeteria serves 247 students in the first lunch period and 369 students in the second lunch period. About how many students are served in both lunch periods?

247 → _____   369 → _____

_____

In which lunch period are more students served?

_____

Problem Solving Strategies 4, SV 0515-4

Name _____ Date _____

MOM! I DON'T HAVE ANYTHING TO WEAR!

Strategy: Make a List

Sometimes it helps to make a list to solve a problem. Put the information in order. Then it will be easy to see how to solve the problem.

STEP 1 **Read the problem.**

Suzy has a red T-shirt and a green blouse. She also has blue jeans and black slacks. How many different combinations of clothing does she have?

STEP 2 **Make a list.**

Start by listing the colors of her tops. Then list the colors of her pants. Draw lines between the lists to match each top with pants. Then write the matches.

Tops	Pants		Matches
red T-shirt ⟶ blue jeans			red T-shirt—blue jeans
green blouse ⟶ black slacks			red T-shirt—black slacks
			green blouse—blue jeans
			green blouse—black slacks

STEP 3 **Count. Solve the problem.**

Count the combinations. There are 4 different ways Suzy can mix her clothes.

Try It! Make a list to solve the problems.

1. A snack shop has white and whole wheat bread. It has tuna, ham, and turkey for sandwiches. How many different kinds of sandwiches can be made?

_____

2. If one more kind of bread is added, how many different kinds of sandwiches can they make?

_____

Is there a pattern?

_____

Unit 2, Addition
Problem Solving Strategies 4, SV 0515-4

Name _____ Date _____

IT'S SNACK TIME. YUMMY!

Strategy: Make a List

STEP 1 ▷ **Read the problem.**

Keisha's favorite snacks are blueberry muffins, oatmeal cookies, and yogurt. Her favorite drinks are milk and juice. How many different combinations of 1 snack and 1 drink can Keisha make?

STEP 2 ▷ **Make a list.**

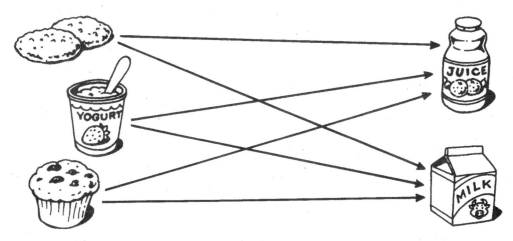

STEP 3 ▷ **Count. Solve the problem.**

Keisha can make 6 different snack combinations.

Try It! Make a list to solve these problems.

1. Samir has a terrier and a poodle. He has brown and white collars for the dogs. How many different ways can he use the collars for his dogs?

_____

2. Kim wants to make a picture. She can use crayons, paints, or markers. She may make her pictures on white paper, yellow paper, or blue paper. How many different ways can she make a picture?

_____

Unit 2, Addition
Problem Solving Strategies 4, SV 0515-4

THERE'S SOMETHING FISHY AT THE AQUARIUM!

Strategy: Choose an Operation

Sometimes a problem does not tell you whether to add or subtract. Read the problem carefully, and decide if you need to add or subtract. Then solve the problem.

STEP 1 **Read the problem.**

Julio's class went to the aquarium on a field trip. In the first tank they saw 67 fish. In the next tank they saw 138 fish. How many fish did they see in both tanks?

STEP 2 **Decide what the problem is asking.**

This problem asks, *"How many fish did they see in both tanks?"*

STEP 3 **Choose an operation.**

Look for key words to help you decide which operation to use. The word *both* signals addition. Add to find how many fish.

STEP 4 **Add. Solve the problem.**

67 + 138 = 205

Julio's class saw 205 fish in both tanks.

Try It! Circle the operation. Solve the problem.

1. Cho counted the students in his school. There were 326 boys and 348 girls. How many students go to Cho's school? Add? Subtract?

   _____

   How does the number of the students in Cho's school compare to your school?

   _____

2. A baker bought 540 pounds of sugar. He used 265 pounds to bake cakes. How much sugar is left? Add? Subtract?

   _____

3. The baker baked 125 cupcakes. He sold 83. How many cupcakes were left? Add? Subtract?

   _____

Unit 2 Review

Strategy
• Make a Table

Show What You Know! Use the table to solve the problems.

The Science Club had a bake sale to buy new equipment for the school's science classes. The club members made and sold 3 types of large cookies: chocolate chip, peanut butter, and sugar. On Saturday, the club sold 847 chocolate chip cookies, 531 peanut butter cookies, and 496 sugar cookies. On Sunday, the club sold 764 chocolate chip cookies, 679 peanut butter cookies, and 517 sugar cookies.

Science Club Bake Sale

	Chocolate Chip Cookies	Peanut Butter Cookies	Sugar Cookies
Saturday			
Sunday			
Totals			

Fill in the table. Then solve the problems.

1. What is the total number of chocolate chip cookies that were sold?

_____

2. What is the total number of peanut butter cookies that were sold?

_____

3. Which type of cookie was most popular?

_____

4. If each cookie costs $1.00, how much money did the Science Club raise by selling cookies on Saturday?

_____

5. How much money did the Science Club raise by selling cookies on Sunday?

_____

Unit 2 Review, page 2

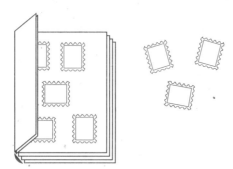

Show What You Know!

Solve each problem. Identify the strategy you used.

1. Danny had a stamp collection. He collected 12 stamps last month and 14 stamps this month. He spent $20 to buy both sets of stamps. How many stamps did he get altogether during the 2 months?

_____

2. Jamal walked 47 miles in June and 53 miles in July. About how many miles did Jamal walk in June and July?

_____

3. Jules and Kitri wanted to ride horses. They went to the stable and saw the horses Smokey, Banjo, and Ringo. How many different combinations of riders and horses are there? Use a list to solve the problem.

_____

4. Penelope made necklaces from glass beads. She had 459 blue beads and 387 red beads. Should Penelope add or subtract to find out how many beads she has? How many beads does Penelope have?

_____

5. Doug traveled 609 miles by bus on Saturday and 753 miles on Sunday. Should he add or subtract to find out how many miles he traveled in two days? How many miles did he travel altogether?

_____

Extension..............

Find the last page number in 2 different textbooks. If you put the books together to make 1 book, how many pages would it have? Make a table to solve the problem.

Name _____ Date _____

FLEX YOUR MATH MUSCLES

A single problem can contain many different problems.

1

The school bus makes four stops each day. At the first stop, 1 boy and 2 girls get on the bus. At the next stop, 2 boys and 3 girls get on. At the third stop, 3 boys and 4 girls get on. Do you see the pattern?

At the last stop before school, how many boys get on the bus?

_____

How many girls get on at the last stop?

_____

Altogether how many children get on the bus?

_____

2

At one school, 267 students ride the bus, 102 ride their bikes, and 68 ride with their parents. Another 32 students walk to school. About how many students go to this school?

_____

3

Here's a tricky one. Mr. and Mrs. Abbott have 3 children, 2 boys and a girl. They would like to have 6 boys and arrange it so each boy has a sister. How many more girls do they have to have for this to happen?

_____

Unit 2, Addition
Problem Solving Strategies 4, SV 0515-4

HEY! HEY! VOTE FOR SHAY! NO! NO! VOTE FOR BO!

Strategy: Make a Table

Sometimes a problem has many facts. Putting the facts in a table can help you see how the facts go together. Then the problem is easier to solve.

Washington Elementary held an election for student council. Complete the table to show the election results.

Fill in the table with these facts:

1. Shay Wilson got 49 votes from the 3rd grade, 39 votes from the 4th grade, and 61 votes from the 5th grade.

2. Bo Rodriquez got 14 votes from the 3rd grade, 57 votes from the 4th grade, and 55 votes from the 5th grade.

Number of Votes

	3rd grade	4th grade	5th grade	Total
Shay				
Bo				

Try It! Use the table to solve these problems.

1. How many more 3rd graders voted for Shay than for Bo?

_____

2. How many more votes did Bo get from the 4th grade than from the 3rd grade?

_____

3. Who got more total votes from the 4th and 5th grades?

4. How many total votes did Shay get from the 4th and 5th grades?

_____

5. How many more votes did the winner get than the loser?

_____

6. Who won the election?

_____

TO THE LIBRARY!

Strategy: Choose an Operation

Sometimes a problem does not tell you whether to add or subtract. Decide what the problem is asking. Do you add or subtract? If it asks you to put together or join groups, then you usually add. If it asks you to take away or compare groups, then you usually subtract. Choose the right operation to solve the problem.

STEP 1 **Read the problem.**
Your school library has 530 CD-ROM titles and 421 filmstrip titles. How many more CD-ROM titles are there?

add?

$$\begin{array}{r} 530 \\ +421 \\ \hline 951 \end{array}$$

STEP 2 **Choose the correct operation.**
To find out how many more, you must subtract.

STEP 3 **Subtract. Solve the problem.**
530 − 421 = 109
There are 109 more CD-ROM titles than filmstrip titles.

subtract?

$$\begin{array}{r} 530 \\ -421 \\ \hline 109 \end{array}$$

Try It! Choose the correct operation. Solve the problem.

1. Tia has a book with 204 pages. There are pictures on 28 pages. How many pages do not have pictures?

add?	subtract?
204	204
+ 28	− 28

2. Raul read for 92 minutes on Monday and 49 minutes on Tuesday. How much longer did he read on Monday than on Tuesday?

add?	subtract?
92	92
+ 49	− 49

3. Chet read one book that had 192 pages. He read another book that had 156 pages. How many pages did he read altogether?

add?	subtract?
192	192
+ 156	− 156

IF YOU CAN'T USE IT, CUT IT OUT!

Strategy: Identify Extra Information

Some problems may give more facts than you need. Read the problem. Decide which facts you need and which are extra. Cross out the extra facts. Use the facts that are left to solve the problem.

STEP 1 ▷ **Read the problem.**

Patti has saved $153 to buy a new basketball hoop and net. One brand costs $96. Another brand costs $105. What is the difference in the cost between the 2 brands?

STEP 2 ▷ **Decide which facts are needed.**

Fact 1: *One brand costs $96.*
Fact 2: *The other brand costs $105.*

STEP 3 ▷ **Decide which facts are extra.**

Patti has saved $153.

STEP 4 ▷ **Subtract. Solve the problem.**

$105 − $96 = $9
One brand costs $9 more than the other.

Try It! Cross out extra information. Then solve each problem.

1. When the Garza family went to the Super Bowl, they drove 741 miles in 2 days. Mr. Garza drove 50 miles per hour all the way. The first day he drove 447 miles. How many miles did he drive the second day?

_____

2. Juan collects sports trading cards. He has 172 baseball cards, 199 football cards, and 88 basketball cards. How many more baseball cards than basketball cards does he have?

_____

EE! EYE! EE! EYE! YO!

Strategy: Use Estimation

You do not always need an exact answer to solve a problem. You can solve some problems by estimating. To estimate, round each number to the same place. Then subtract the rounded numbers.

Old MacDonald raises cows on his farm. In April his cows produced 1,316 gallons of milk. He sold 918 gallons of milk. About how many gallons were left?

 Estimate to the nearest hundred.
$1,316 \rightarrow 1,300$ $918 \rightarrow 900$

 Subtract. Solve the problem.
$1,300 - 900 = 400$
About 400 gallons were left.

Try It! Round to the nearest hundred, then solve.

1. Old MacDonald drove 6,322 miles in his green pick-up truck. He drove 4,588 miles in his blue car. About how many more miles did he drive in his truck than in his car?

   _____

2. Termites ate Old MacDonald's fence posts! He must replace them. (The posts, not the termites.) He bought 2,305 fence posts. He replaced 917 posts. About how many fence posts are left to replace?

   _____

3. On his farm (really, it's a ranch), he had 12,642 head of cattle. He took 11,011 on a cattle drive. About how many head of cattle remained on the ranch?

   _____

4. Of the 26,341 acres of land on his ranch, he has cattle on 24,679 acres. About how many acres do not have cattle on them?

   _____

Name _____ Date _____

WHAT A SPORT!

Strategy: Use a Graph

Students at your school voted for their favorite sports. The bar graph shows the number of votes each sport received.

To read a bar graph, line up the top of each bar with the number on the left.

Students' Favorite Sports

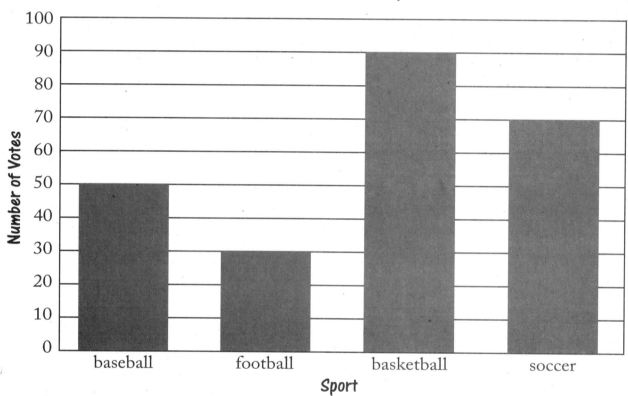

Try It! Use the graph to solve the problems.

1. What is the favorite sport?

_____

2. How many more votes did the favorite sport receive than the next favorite?

_____

3. Each student had 1 vote. How many students voted?

_____

4. How many more students voted for soccer than for football?

_____

Unit 3, Subtraction
Problem Solving Strategies 4, SV 0515-4

REUBEN IS A SLUGGER!

Strategy: Work Backward

Sometimes it helps to start at the end of a problem and work backward.

 Read the problem.

Reuben has scored 142 runs for his team so far this year. He scored 12 runs yesterday. How many runs did he score before yesterday?

STEP 2 **List the facts.**

Fact 1: *Reuben scored 142 runs.*
Fact 2: *He scored 12 runs yesterday.*

STEP 3 **Subtract. Solve the problem.**

142 − 12 = 130
Reuben scored 130 runs before yesterday.

Try It! Work backward to solve these problems.

1. Shari gave out 59 programs before the game started. By the time the game ended, she had given out 217 programs. How many programs did she give out during the game?

_____

2. Valencia sold 48 bags of peanuts at the ball game. She has 76 more bags to sell. How many bags of peanuts did she have when she started selling?

_____

3. If Valencia earned $96 selling peanuts at the ball game (Question #2), how much was each bag?

_____

4. After Valencia has sold all of the bags of peanuts, will she have $200?

_____

How much more or less than $200 will she have?

_____

5. Sid is a pitcher on Reuben's team. He pitched in both games of a doubleheader. Altogether, he threw 112 pitches in the two games. In the first game, Sid threw 84 pitches. How many pitches did he throw in the second game?

_____

Name _____   Date _____

FOR THE BIRDS!

Strategy: Identify Substeps

Sometimes a problem has more than 1 part.

STEP 1 **Read the problem.**
Allegra has a birdhouse in her backyard. In June she saw 57 birds visit the birdhouse. She saw 16 fewer birds in May. How many birds visited the house in both months?

STEP 2 **Solve the first part.**
Find the number of birds she saw in May.
$57 - 16 = 41$

STEP 3 **Solve the second part.**
Find the number of birds she saw in both months.
$57 + 41 = 98$

Try It! Use a two-part plan to solve these problems.

1. Pablo bought binoculars for $7.00 and a book on birds for $5.00. He gave the clerk $15.00. How much change did he get back?

_____

2. Rosa photographed 144 birds. There were 62 cardinals and 54 sparrows. The rest of the birds were robins. How many robins did Rosa photograph?

_____

3. Rosa bought 50 lbs of bird feed. She used 17 lbs the first week and 15 lbs the second week. How much does she have for next week?

_____

4. Pablo bought supplies for $213. He used $75 for bird feed and $15 for sugar. If he spent the rest of the money for bird feeders, how much did he spend for bird feeders?

_____

Problem Solving Strategies 4, SV 0515-4

Unit 3 Review

Show What You Know! Solve each problem.

Kelly's Car Lot has 37 blue cars, 28 green cars, and 15 white cars. The sales team sold 12 blue cars, 7 green cars, and 5 white cars.

	Blue	Green	White
Number of Cars on Lot			
Number of Cars Sold			

1. a. Put the facts in the table.

   b. To begin with, how many more blue cars than green cars were on the lot?

   _____

2. To begin with, how many more green cars than white cars were on the lot?

   _____

3. How many more blue cars than white cars were sold?

   _____

4. How many more green cars than white cars were sold?

   _____

5. How many blue cars were still on the lot after 12 were sold?

   _____

6. How many green cars were left on the lot after 7 were sold?

   _____

7. How many white cars were left on the lot after 5 were sold?

   _____

Unit 3 Review, page 2

Strategies

- Choose an Operation
- Identify Extra Information
- Use Estimation
- Use a Graph
- Work Backward
- Identify Substeps

Show What You Know!

1. Veronica had $28. She bought $17 worth of groceries. Would you add or subtract to find out how much money she had after she bought her groceries? How much money did she have left after buying her groceries?

_____

2. In a grocery store, there are 45 cans of corn and 27 cans of string beans on the shelves. Customers buy 17 cans of corn. How many cans of corn does the store have left?

_____

3. Tyler earned 1,759 points playing the first round of a video game. He earned 2,398 points playing the second round. Rounding to the nearest hundred, about how many points did Tyler earn altogether?

_____

Solve each problem. Identify the strategy you used.

4. In the morning, Lori handed out 26 programs for the school play to other fourth-grade students. By the end of the school day, she had handed out 193 programs. How many programs did she hand out in the afternoon?

_____

5. A family was going to drive 747 miles to see the Grand Canyon. It was a 2-day trip. They drove 402 miles the first day. How many miles did they drive the second day?

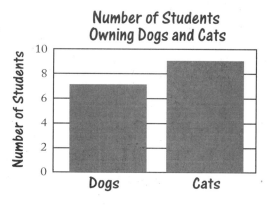

Number of Students Owning Dogs and Cats

6. Do more students own dogs or cats?

_____

FLEX YOUR MATH MUSCLES

1

30 days have September, April,
June, and November. All the rest
have 31, except poor February,
with only 28. But in a leap year,
it has 29 days! How many months
have 28 days?

_____

(Be careful, and think ahead!)

2

Ugh and Duh are cavemen. They use sticks for numbers. A single stick
stands for 1; 2 sticks stand for 2; and so on. Ugh has a lot of trouble
learning how to add and subtract. One day, he asks Duh for help with
his homework. Ugh has placed 11 sticks like this:

"Something is wrong," says Duh.
"The sticks read $2 - 4 = 2$."

You can solve the problem by
moving just 1 stick. Sure you can.
You're smarter than a caveman!
Which stick do you move? Draw your answer in the box.

Name _____ Date _____

SATURDAY NIGHT AT THE MOVIES

Strategy: Choose an Operation

Some problems do not tell you whether to add, subtract, multiply, or divide. Read the problem carefully. Decide what the problem is asking you to do. Choose an operation, then solve the problem.

STEP 1 ▷ Read the problem.
Erica has 3 boxes of microwave popcorn to share while watching movies with friends. Each box has 4 bags of popcorn inside. If each of her friends eats 1 bag, will Erica have enough popcorn for 10 people?

STEP 2 ▷ Decide what the problem is asking.
You need to find out how many bags of popcorn she has altogether. *Altogether* signals to find a sum or product.

STEP 3 ▷ Choose an operation.
To solve the problem, you can add 4 three times. With equal parts, it is faster to multiply 4×3.

STEP 4 ▷ Add or multiply. Solve the problem.
$4 + 4 + 4 = 12$ *OR* $4 \times 3 = 12$ 12 is greater than 10.
Erica has enough popcorn!

Try It!   Choose the correct operation, then solve.

1. Adrienne has 2 empty shelves in her bookcase. Each shelf holds 28 videos. How many videos can she put on the shelves? Circle the correct operation.

$$\begin{array}{r} 2\,8 \\ \times \quad 2 \\ \hline \end{array} \qquad 2\overline{)28}$$

Does she have room for 50 videos?

_____

2. Mr. Watts works 9 hours a day at the theater. He works 6 days a week. How many hours does he work each week?

_____

The average work week is 40 hours. How much more does Mr. Watts work?

_____

Problem Solving Strategies 4, SV 0515-4

Name _____ Date _____

HOORAY!! THE CIRCUS IS COMING TO TOWN!

Strategy: Use Estimation

You do not always need an exact answer to solve a problem. Some problems can be solved by estimating. Round each number to the same place. Then solve the problem using the rounded numbers.

STEP 1 **Read the problem.**
Shontal sold 17 T-shirts at the circus for $8 each. Her goal was to sell $100 worth of T-shirts. Did she reach her goal?

STEP 2 **Identify the important facts.**
Shontal sold 17 T-shirts. They cost $8 each. She wanted to sell $100 worth of T-shirts.

STEP 3 **Round all numbers.**
17 Æ 20 $8 Æ $10

STEP 4 **Multiply. Solve the problem.**
20 × $10 = $200
$200 is more than $100. Shontal met her goal.

Try It!   Use estimation to solve these problems.

1. There are 12 dogs in the show. Each dog is 19 inches long. If the dogs are put end to end, about how many inches long would they be in all?

_____

About how many feet is that?

_____

2. The school band wants to wear gold-braided hats for the circus parade. The band has $480. Is there enough money to buy fancy hats for 46 students if each hat costs $13?

_____

3. If the fierce lion sleeps 16 hours a day, about how many hours will it sleep in 10 days?

_____

Unit 4, Multiplication
Problem Solving Strategies 4, SV 0515-4

PIZZA, PIZZA!! WHO'S GOT THE PIZZA?

Strategy: Make a Table

Sometimes a problem has many facts. Organizing the facts in a table helps show how the facts go together. You can use the table to solve the problem.

STEP 1 **Read the problem.**

Jack's Pizza Shop is doing well. On Saturday he sold 45 cheese pizzas, 36 sausage pizzas, and 64 pepperoni pizzas. Cheese pizzas cost $2.00 each, sausage pizzas cost $4.00 each, and pepperoni pizzas cost $5.00 each. How much money did Jack take in on Saturday?

STEP 2 **List the facts.**

Fact 1: *On Saturday he sold 45 cheese pizzas, 36 sausage pizzas, and 64 pepperoni pizzas.*

Fact 2: *Cheese pizzas cost $2.00, sausage pizzas cost $4.00, and pepperoni pizzas cost $5.00.*

STEP 3 **Make a table.**

		Cheese	Sausage	Pepperoni
Saturday Sales		45	36	64
Cheese	$2	$2 × 45 = A		
Sausage	$4		$4 × 36 = B	
Pepperoni	$5			$5 × 64 = C
Totals		A	B	C

STEP 4 **Add. Solve the problem.**

Add together the totals.   A + B + C = ?

Try It!   Use the table to solve the problem.

1. How much money did Jack take in on Saturday?

_____

2. On which kind of pizza did he take in the most money?

_____

Name _____ Date _____

PIZZA, PIZZA!! WHO'S GOT THE PIZZA?, part 2

Strategy: Make a Table

Try It! Complete this table to solve Problem 1.

		Cheese	Sausage	Pepperoni
Sunday Sales		15	29	38
Cheese	$2	$2 × ? = A		
Sausage	$4		$4 × ? = B	
Pepperoni	$5			$5 × ? = C
Totals		A	B	C

1. On Sunday, Jack sold 15 cheese pizzas, 29 sausage pizzas, and 38 pepperoni pizzas.

   How much money did Jack take in on Sunday? _____

   Did he take in more money on Saturday or Sunday? _____

   Which pizza brought in the most money for the 2 days? _____

Try It! Make your own tables to solve these problems.

2. Jack used 6 tomatoes, 3 onions, and 12 cups of shredded cheese to make pizzas. He made 3 pizzas. How much of each ingredient did he use for each pizza?

   _____

   _____

   _____

   What else do you think he should put on the pizzas?

   _____

3. Jack wants to buy in-line skates with the money he earns selling pizza. He earns $5.00 an hour. On Friday he worked 6 hours. On Saturday he worked 8 hours. On Sunday he worked 7 hours. How much money did Jack earn this weekend?

   _____

"RAH, RAH, RAH! GO TEAM!"

Strategy: Find a Pattern

Some problems can be solved by finding a pattern. Read the problem carefully. Look for a pattern. Write the rule that makes and completes the pattern. Then solve the problem.

 Read the problem.
What are the next two numbers in this pattern?
3, 9, 27, . . .

 Determine the relationship.

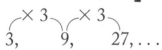
$$\overset{\times 3}{\frown} \quad \overset{\times 3}{\frown}$$
3,   9,   27, . . .

 Write the rule.
Multiply by 3.

Multiply. Solve the problem.
$27 \times 3 = 81$ $81 \times 3 = 243$
The next two numbers are 81 and 243.

Try It!   Find a pattern to solve these problems.

1. Tiffany's teammates have jerseys numbered 20, 25, and 35. Tiffany's jersey is missing. What is her number? Number the jerseys below.

Fill in the blanks with the next 2 numbers in each sequence.

2. 2, 5, 8, 11, _____, _____

3. 198, 297, 396, _____, _____

4. 60, 63, 58, 61, _____, _____

5. 42, 49, 56, _____, _____

Name _____ Date _____

"PLAY BALL!"

Strategy: Work Backward

When given the outcome, work backward to solve the problem. Read carefully to find clues. Then work backward.

STEP 1 ▷ Read the problem.

Mrs. Perez gave her 5 basketball players the same number of warm-up exercises. After Janelle did 2 exercises, she had 7 left to finish. Altogether how many warm-up exercises did the team do?

STEP 2 ▷ List the clues.

Clue A: *There are 5 basketball team players.*
Clue B: *They all have the same number of warm-up exercises.*
Clue C: *Janelle has already done 2 warm-up exercises.*
Clue D: *She has 7 warm-up exercises left to finish.*

STEP 3 ▷ Work backward.

Start at the end of the problem.

- Add the number of exercises Janelle has left to the exercises she has done. $7 + 2 = 9$
- Multiply the number of Janelle's warm-up exercises by the number of players. $9 \times 5 = 45$

STEP 4 ▷ Multiply. Solve the problem.

Altogether the team did 45 exercises.

Try It! Work backward to solve the problems.

1. The golf coach gave 6 players the same number of golf balls. After Tim hit 4 golf balls, he had 3 left. How many golf balls in all did the coach give the players?

_____

2. Johnny has 30 pages left to read in his sports almanac. Yesterday he read twice that many pages. The first day he read 5 more pages than yesterday. How many pages are in his almanac?

_____

Name _____ Date _____

SHOWING SCHOOL SPIRIT

Strategy: Make a List

Sometimes it helps to make a list to solve a multiplication problem. When you put the information in a list in an organized way, it is easy to see how to solve the problem.

STEP 1 ▷ Read the problem.

Thorp School sells shirts, pants, and shorts. Each comes in school colors, blue or gold. How many combinations of outfits are there?

STEP 2 ▷ Make a list.

List each color of shirt in the left column. Write each color of pants in the next column. Draw lines to match each shirt with each pair of pants. Write the combinations.

Shirts	Pants
blue shirt	blue pants
	gold pants
gold shirt	blue shorts
	gold shorts

Combinations

blue shirt/blue pants
blue shirt/gold pants
blue shirt/blue shorts
blue shirt/gold shorts
gold shirt/blue pants
gold shirt/gold pants
gold shirt/blue shorts
gold shirt/gold shorts

STEP 3 ▷ Count or multiply. Solve the problem.

Count the different matches.

Shortcut! Multiply:

2	kinds of shirts
× 4	kinds of pants
8	different matches

Try It! Make a list or multiply to solve.

1. Paige has pink, blue, and black leotards. She has white and pink ballet slippers. How many different combinations of leotards and slippers can she wear?

_____

Name _____ Date _____

Unit 4 Review

Strategies
- Choose an Operation
- Use Estimation
- Find a Pattern
- Work Backward
- Make a List

Show What You Know!

Solve each problem. Identify the strategy you used.

1. Darla planted 8 tomato plants in each of 4 rows. Would you multiply or divide to find out how many tomato plants she planted altogether? How many tomato plants did she plant altogether?

_____

2. Fill in the blanks with the next 2 numbers in the sequence.

8, 16, 24, _____, _____

3. A store sold 21 radios in 3 days. The store sold the same number of radios each day. How many radios did the store sell each day?

_____

4. A museum had 23 visitors every hour on Monday. The museum was open for 8 hours. About how many visitors came to the museum on Monday?

_____

5. Pedro has red, blue, and green paint for his model trains. He has an engine, a passenger car, and a caboose. He painted each model train car all one color. He uses each color of paint only one time. How many different combinations of paint and model train cars can he make? Make a list to solve the problem.

_____

Name _____ Date _____

Unit 4 Review, page 2

Strategy: Make a Table

A candy shop sold boxes of chocolates. On Saturday, the shop sold 64 boxes of plain chocolates, 56 boxes of chocolates with nuts, and 40 boxes of chocolates with different kinds of fillings.

	Plain Chocolates	Chocolates with Nuts	Chocolates with Fillings
Saturday Sales	64 boxes	56 boxes	40 boxes
Box of Plain Chocolates ($3 per box)			
Box of Chocolates with Nuts ($5 per box)			
Box of Chocolates with Fillings ($4 per box)			

Show What You Know!

Complete the table. Use the table to solve each problem.

1. On Saturday, how much money did the shop make selling plain chocolates?

_____

2. How much money did the shop make selling chocolates with nuts?

_____

3. How much money did the shop make selling chocolates with fillings?

_____

4. On Saturday, what was the total amount of money the candy shop made by selling boxes of chocolate?

_____

5. Which type of chocolates did the candy store sell the most boxes of?

_____

6. Which type of chocolates made the most money for the candy store?

_____

Problem Solving Strategies 4, SV 0515-4

Name _____ Date _____

1

Poor Flex. He is having a very difficult time with his multiplication. Please help Flex find the product of these numbers. You can do it!

(Hint: Look at the whole problem before you start multiplying.)

$27 \times 567 \times 18 \times 943 \times 0 =$ _____

2

This multiplication problem gives the answer. You will have to figure out the problem! A, B, and C are single digit numbers that you have to find. There is more than one way to do this. Try and see!

$A + (B \times C) = 27$

A = _____ B = _____ C = _____

3

Pablo and Flex are riding their bikes on a flat road that is 20 miles long. They start at opposite ends and ride toward each other at a speed of 10 miles per hour. A bee flies back and forth from Flex's bike to Pablo's at 15 miles per hour until they meet in the middle. How far will the bee have flown when they meet?

_____

(Hint: Think about how much time it will take Pablo and Flex to meet.)

4

Do you know what a dozen is? A dozen is 12 of anything. A dozen eggs is 12 eggs. A dozen widgets is 12 widgets. If there are 12 one-cent stamps in a dozen, how many two-cent stamps are in a dozen?

_____

Problem Solving Strategies 4, SV 0515-4

YANKEE DOODLE COMES TO TOWN!

Strategy: Choose an Operation

Sometimes a problem does not tell you whether to add, subtract, multiply, or divide. Read the problem carefully, and decide what the problem is asking you to do. Choose an operation, then solve the problem.

STEP 1 ▷ **Read the problem.**
Mr. Johnson has 36 American flags in 6 boxes. If each box holds the same number of flags, how many flags are in each box?

STEP 2 ▷ **Decide what the problem is asking.**
In this problem, the question "how many . . . in each" is asking you to find equal parts.

STEP 3 ▷ **Choose an operation.**
Look for key words to help you decide which operation to use. "How many . . . in each" signals division. To solve this problem, you must divide.

STEP 4 ▷ **Divide. Solve the problem.**
$36 \div 6 = 6$
There are 6 American flags in each box.

Try It! Choose the correct operation to solve these problems.

1. Mr. Wojak is cutting watermelon at the 4th of July picnic. He serves 12 people from each watermelon. If there are 60 people at the picnic, how many watermelons will he need?

_____

2. A case has 144 sparklers. There are 24 children at the picnic. Each child gets an equal number of sparklers. How many sparklers does each child get?

_____

OLYMPICS, HERE WE COME!

Strategy: Work Backward

When given the outcome, work backward to solve the problem. Read carefully to find the clues. Then work backward.

STEP 1 **Read the problem.**

Danielle, Genie, and Zoe take gymnastics. Danielle can do 4 more cartwheels than Genie. Genie can do half as many cartwheels as Zoe. Zoe does 8 cartwheels. How many cartwheels does Danielle do?

STEP 2 **List the clues.**

Clue 1: *Danielle can do 4 more cartwheels than Genie.*

Clue 2: *Genie can do half as many cartwheels as Zoe.*

Clue 3: *Zoe does 8 cartwheels.*

STEP 3 **Work backward. Solve the problem.**

Start at the end of the problem and work backward.

- *Genie can do half as many cartwheels as Zoe.* $8 \div 2 = 4$
  Genie does 4 cartwheels.

- *Danielle can do 4 more cartwheels than Genie.* $4 + 4 = 8$
  Danielle does 8 cartwheels.

Try It!   Work backward to solve these problems.

1. Raul knows 2 fewer wrestling holds than Jeff. Jeff knows 3 more than Ian. Ian knows 9 holds. How many wrestling holds does Raul know?

_____

Who knows the most wrestling holds?

_____

2. Today Alfred swam 30 practice laps in the pool. Yesterday he swam 10 laps fewer than today. Tomorrow he will swim 10 more than today. How many practice laps will Alfred have done in the 3 days?

_____

AS EASY AS PIE!

Strategy: Find a Pattern

The answer to a problem may be found by recognizing a pattern. Read the problem carefully. Look for a pattern. Then write the rule that makes and completes the pattern. Solve the problem.

STEP 1 ▷ **Read the problem.**

Mark made pies for a bake sale. He made 96 pies the first week, 48 pies the second week, 24 pies the third week, and 12 pies the fourth week. How many pies did he make the fifth week and sixth week?

STEP 2 ▷ **Determine the relationship.**

$$\div 2 \quad \div 2 \quad \div 2$$
$$96, \quad 48, \quad 24, \quad 12, \ldots$$

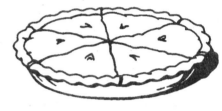

STEP 3 ▷ **Write the rule.**

Divide by 2.

STEP 4 ▷ **Divide. Solve the problem.**

$12 \div 2 = 6 \quad 6 \div 2 = 3$

Mark made 6 pies the fifth week and 3 pies the sixth week.

Try It! Find a pattern to solve these problems.

1. The Smith's Ice Cream Shop is celebrating their third anniversary with a special giveaway. Each time someone orders ice cream, Mr. Smith gives away free toppings! LaNelle ordered 9 scoops and received 3 free toppings. Willy ordered 6 scoops and received 2 free toppings. If Emil orders 12 scoops of ice cream, how many free toppings will he get?

_____

2. To celebrate the anniversary, the Smiths sponsor a race. Their daughter Sandra is Runner C. Runner A is number 256, Runner B is number 64, and Runner D is number 4. What is Sandra's number?

_____

3. The first-place winner in the marathon gets $250; second gets $50; third gets $10. How much does the fourth-place runner get?

_____

Name _____ Date _____

WE HAVE A MYSTERY TO SOLVE!

Strategy: Division Practice

Cory received this secret message from his friend Jerry. Can you decode the message?
Write the letter under each problem with the matching answer.

A	B	C	E	F	H	I	M	O	R	T	W
18	3	15	4	42	21	6	13	9	5	12	0

___ ___ ___ ___ ___ ___

First Word

$27 \div 9 = $ ____

$16 \div 4 = $ ____

$0 \div 13 = $ ____

$36 \div 2 = $ ____

$125 \div 25 = $ ____

$48 \div 12 = $ ____

___ ___ ___

Second Word

$45 \div 5 = $ ____

$126 \div 3 = $ ____

___ ___ ___

Third Word

$72 \div 6 = $ ____

$105 \div 5 = $ ____

$64 \div 16 = $ ____

___ ___ ___ ___ ___

Fourth Word

$143 \div 11 = $ ____

$234 \div 13 = $ ____

$145 \div 29 - $ ____

$75 \div 5 = $ ____

$441 \div 21 = $ ____

___ ___ ___ ___

Fifth Word

$63 \div 3 = $ ____

$54 \div 3 = $ ____

$40 \div 8 = $ ____

$92 \div 23 = $ ____

The secret message says:

_____

Unit 5, Division
Problem Solving Strategies 4, SV 0515-4

Name _____ Date _____

APRIL SHOWERS BRING MAY FLOWERS

Strategy: Use a Graph

A graph is a special table of facts. A bar graph contains information in the shape of bars. The length of a bar represents a number. To read a bar graph, match the bars with the numbers.

STEP 1 **Read the problem.**

The florist keeps track of how many roses she orders. How many more roses did she order in May, compared to June and to October?

STEP 2 **Read the graph.**

A. Find the labels for May, June, and October at the bottom of the graph.

B. Move your finger to the top of the bar for each of those months. Then move across to the left to find the number of roses she ordered.

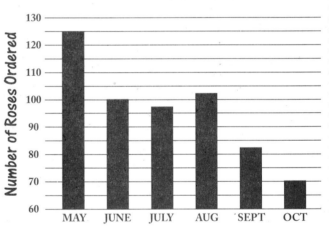

Roses Ordered, May–October

STEP 3 **Write the facts.**

Fact 1: *In May she ordered 125 roses.*

Fact 2: *In June she ordered 100 roses.*

Fact 3: *In October she ordered 70 roses.*

STEP 4 **Subtract. Solve the problem.**

Subtract to find how many more she ordered in May than in June and in October.

$125 - 100 = 25$ In May she ordered 25 more roses than in June.

$125 - 70 = 55$ In May she ordered 55 more roses than in October.

Name _____ Date _____

GOING TO THE THEATER

Strategy: Make a Graph

Sometimes you need to gather information before making a bar graph.

Try It! Use division to find out how many chairs are in each row. Then use the information to make your bar graph.

Mrs. Wilfong arranges chairs differently for each night of Summer Theater. A wide row with many chairs makes more stage space. A narrow row with few chairs makes more aisle space. The gymnastics show needs the most stage space. The comedy act needs the most aisle space.

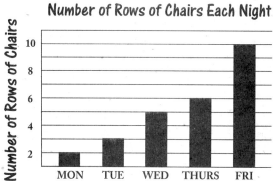

Number of Rows of Chairs Each Night

Last week Mrs. Wilfong used 30 chairs. On Monday she made 2 rows, on Tuesday she made 3 rows, on Wednesday she made 5 rows, on Thursday she made 6 rows, and on Friday she made 10 rows.

1. How many chairs were in each row on . . .

Monday? _____   Tuesday? _____

Wednesday? _____   Thursday? _____

Friday? _____

2. Which night had the rows with the most chairs?

_____

3. Which night had the rows with the fewest chairs?

_____

4. The gymnastics show was on which night?

_____

5. The comedy act was on which night?

_____

Problem Solving Strategies 4, SV 0515-4

Name _____ Date _____

FUNDRAISING IS FUN!

Strategy: Use Estimation

Often you do not need an exact answer to solve a problem. Some problems can be solved by estimating. Round each number to the same place. Then solve the problem using the rounded numbers.

 Read the problem.
To raise money for the school field trip, Noriko made $104 washing cars. She washed 19 cars. About how much did each person spend on a car wash?

 List the facts.
Fact 1: *Noriko made $104 washing cars.*
Fact 2: *She washed 19 cars.*

STEP 3 **Round each number.**
$104 Æ $100   19 Æ 20

STEP 4 **Divide. Solve the problem.**
$100 ÷ 20 = $5
Each person spent about $5 for a car wash.

Try It!   Use estimation to solve these problems.

1. Ramon sold 32 necklaces. He made $61. About how much did he make for each necklace?

_____

2. Altogether, about how many necklaces will Ramon have to sell to pay for his $89 field trip?

_____

3. Jessye sold 12 hair ribbons at a craft fair to raise money for her field trip. She made $64. About how much did each hair ribbon cost?

_____

4. If Jessye still needs $36, about how many more hair ribbons must she sell?

_____

Name _____   Date _____

Unit 5 Review

Show What You Know!

Solve each problem. Identify the strategy you used.

1. On Monday, a pet store had 64 bags of cat food on the shelf. On Tuesday, there were only 56 bags left. On Wednesday, there were 48 bags left. If this pattern continues, how many bags of cat food will be left on Thursday and Friday?

_____

2. Ms. Rodriguez worked for 5 hours on Monday and 5 hours on Tuesday. She earned $150 in the 2 days. How much did Ms. Rodriguez get paid for each hour that she worked?

_____

3. Mr. Chan made hot dogs for 36 people at a cookout. There are 12 hot dog buns in each package. How many packages of hot dog buns did Mr. Chan need?

_____

4. Petula walked her neighbors' dogs to earn money. She made $2 for each dog she walked. On June 10, she made $24. How many dogs did she walk on that date?

_____

Unit 5 Review, page 2

Strategies
- Use a Graph
- Make a Graph

Show What You Know!

Solve each problem. Identify the strategy you used.

Heather and Vanyel put library books on some new bookcases. They put 144 books on a bookcase with 6 shelves. They put 150 books on a bookcase with 5 shelves. They put 112 books on a bookcase with 4 shelves. For each bookcase, they put the same number of books on each shelf. However, the number of books per shelf varied from bookcase to bookcase.

Complete the graph to show how many books there were per shelf for each bookshelf.

1. How many books went on each shelf of the bookcase with 6 shelves?

_____

2. How many books went on each shelf of the bookcase with 5 shelves?

_____

3. How many books went on each shelf of the bookcase with 4 shelves?

_____

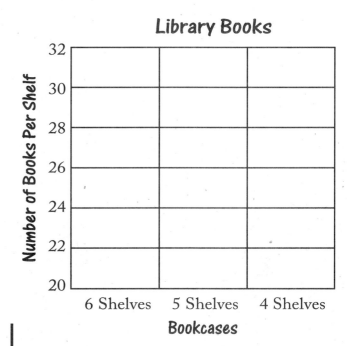

4. Which bookcase had the most books per shelf?

_____

5. How many more books were on each shelf of the bookcase with 4 shelves than on the bookcase with 6 shelves?

_____

Unit 5, Division
Problem Solving Strategies 4, SV 0515-4

Name _____ Date _____

FLEX YOUR MATH MUSCLES

1

Flex has 6 apples, and there are 7 people at his house. He wants to share the apples equally. How can he do this? (This is a pretty sneaky way of dividing stuff!)

_____

2

The lights went out at Flex's house! He had to find his socks and shoes in total darkness. In his dresser drawer, he had a dozen loose black socks and 12 loose white socks. What is the smallest number of socks he could take out of the drawer to be sure he held a matching pair?

_____

3

The Sunshine Express train goes from New York City to Miami. The Big Town Limited goes from Miami to New York City on the same track. The Sunshine Express travels at 90 miles per hour, and the Big Town Limited travels at 60 miles per hour. If they leave at the same time, which train is closer to New York City when they meet?

_____

STOCKING UP ON SCHOOL SUPPLIES

Strategy: Choose an Operation

Some problems do not tell you whether to add, subtract, multiply, or divide. Read the problem carefully. Decide what the problem is asking you to do. Then solve the problem.

EXAMPLE A

STEP 1 ▷ **Read the problem.**
Jason has 4 boxes of striped pencils. There are 18 pencils in each box. How many pencils does Jason have altogether?

STEP 2 ▷ **Decide what the problem is asking.**
This problem asks, "How many pencils does Jason have altogether?"

STEP 3 ▷ **Choose an operation.**
Look for key words to help you decide which operation to use. The word *altogether* signals addition or multiplication. Find a sum or product. To solve the problem, you could add 18 four times. Since there are equal parts, it is faster to multiply 4×18.

STEP 4 ▷ **Add or multiply. Solve the problem.**
$18 + 18 + 18 + 18 = 72$ *OR* $18 \times 4 = 72$ Jason has 72 pencils.

EXAMPLE B

STEP 1 ▷ **Read the problem.**
Mrs. Kutsuwa has 42 folders for her students. Each student needs 2 folders. How many students does she have?

STEP 2 ▷ **Decide what the problem is asking.**
This problem asks, "How many students does she have?" You must find equal parts.

STEP 3 ▷ **Choose an operation.**
To solve, you must divide.

STEP 4 ▷ **Divide. Solve the problem.**
$42 \div 2 = 21$ Mrs. Kutsuwa has 21 students.

STOCKING UP ON SCHOOL SUPPLIES, part 2

Strategy: Choose an Operation

Some problems do not tell you whether to add, subtract, multiply, or divide. Read the problem carefully. Decide what the problem is asking you to do. Then solve the problem.

Try It! Choose the correct operation, then solve these problems.

1. There are 13 cans of blue paint, 9 cans of red paint, and 11 cans of green paint on a shelf. How many cans of paint are on the shelf?

_____

2. There are 5 test tubes in a box. The science class needs 45 test tubes for an experiment. How many boxes do they need?

_____

3. The librarian counted 98 biographies in the school library. For their book reports, 26 students each checked out a biography. How many biographies were left in the library?

_____

4. There are 8 map colors in a box. Each student needs 4 colors for a map. If there are 36 students in the class, how many boxes of map colors does the class need?

_____

5. Mr. Price has to pack a total of 48 calculators in the fourth-grade math kits. He will make 8 kits. How many calculators will he put in each kit?

_____

6. D'Shawn has 32 beakers. She fills 17 beakers with water. How many beakers are left for her to fill?

_____

7. The school yearbook has 64 pages. The introduction takes 7 pages. Student photos are on 32 pages. How many pages are left to use for student news and advertising?

_____

8. There are 54 microscopes for the science classes at the school. There are 9 science classes. How many microscopes does each class have?

_____

SUMMER COOKING CLASS

Strategy: Write a Number Sentence

A number sentence shows how numbers are related to each other. Read the problem and find the clues. Write a number sentence. To solve the problem, you may need to work backward.

STEP 1 ▸ **Read the problem.**
Niljia used 3 teaspoons of water in her recipe. She also used some milk. Altogether she used 7 teaspoons of liquid. How much milk did she use?

STEP 2 ▸ **List the clues.**
Clue 1: *Niljia used 3 teaspoons of water.*
Clue 2: *She also used some milk.*
Clue 3: *Altogether she used 7 teaspoons of liquid.*

STEP 3 ▸ **Write a number sentence.**
teaspoons of milk + teaspoons of water = total teaspoons of liquid
$$? + 3 = 7$$

STEP 4 ▸ **Subtract. Solve the problem.**
To find the missing number, work backward.
$? = 7 - 3$ Since $7 - 3 = 4$, Niljia used 4 teaspoons of milk.

Try It! Write number sentences to solve these problems.

1. Mr. Molina bought cookbooks for his students. He got 32 cookbooks. If each cooking class has 8 students, how many classes does Mr. Molina teach?

_____

If each class lasts for 13 weeks, how many groups of students does he have in a year?

_____

2. Darlene has grilled 9 hot dogs at her summer party. Altogether she has to grill 16 hot dogs. How many more does she have to grill?

_____

If there are 8 hot dogs in each package, how many packages will she need?

_____

Name _____   Date _____

A DAY AT THE RINK

Strategy: Work Backward

When given the outcome, start at the end of the problem. Read the problem carefully, and find the clues. Then work backward to solve the problem.

STEP 1 ▷ **Read the problem.**

Hal did 8 spins during ice skating practice. Scott did half as many spins as Hal. Ricardo did 2 more spins than Scott. How many spins each did Scott and Ricardo do?

STEP 2 ▷ **List the clues.**

Clue 1: *Hal did 8 spins.*
Clue 2: *Scott did half as many spins as Hal.*
Clue 3: *Ricardo did 2 more spins than Scott.*

STEP 3 ▷ **Solve the problem.**

Start at the end of the problem and work backward.
Scott did half as many spins as Hal. $8 \div 2 = 4$ Scott did 4 spins.
Ricardo did 2 more spins than Scott. $4 + 2 = 6$ Ricardo did 6 spins.

Try It!   Work backward to solve these problems.

1. On Saturday morning Monique had $20.00 before going to the ice rink. She spent $6.00 for her lesson, $1.50 for skate rental, and $0.50 for a soda while she was there. She had $7.00 when she came home. How much had she spent before going to the ice rink?

_____

2. Jenny won a jar of jelly beans in a skating contest. If you subtract 68 from the total number of jelly beans in the jar, the answer is 721. How many jelly beans are in Jenny's jar?

_____

How could you estimate the number of jelly beans in the jar?

_____

_____

Name _____ Date _____

ROY THE WRANGLER

Strategy: Make a Table

Sometimes a problem has many facts. Organizing the facts in a table helps show how the facts go together. Use the table to solve the problem.

STEP 1 ▸ **Read the problem.**

Rowdy Roy works on a ranch. On Monday he ropes 6 horses, 9 sheep, and 7 steers. On Wednesday he ropes 8 horses, 10 sheep, and 13 steers. On Friday Roy ropes 4 horses, 12 sheep, and 18 steers. How many more animals does Roy rope on Friday than on Monday?

STEP 2 ▸ **List the facts.**

Fact 1: *On Monday Roy ropes 6 horses, 9 sheep, and 7 steers.*
Fact 2: *On Wednesday Roy ropes 8 horses, 10 sheep, and 13 steers.*
Fact 3: *On Friday Roy ropes 4 horses, 12 sheep, and 18 steers.*

STEP 3 ▸ **Make a table.**

	Monday	Wednesday	Friday
horses	6	8	4
sheep	9	10	12
steers	7	13	18
Totals	A	B	C

STEP 4 ▸ **Add and subtract. Solve the problem.**

Add the numbers in the columns, then subtract.
$A = 6 + 9 + 7 = 22$ $C = 4 + 12 + 18 = 34$ $C - A = 34 - 22 = 12$
Roy ropes 12 more animals on Friday than he does on Monday.

Try It! Use the table above to solve these problems.

1. How many animals does Roy rope on Wednesday? _____

2. How many horses does Roy rope altogether? _____

How many sheep in all? _____   How many steers in all? _____

Problem Solving Strategies 4, SV 0515-4

DINOSAUR DILEMMAS

Strategy: Guess and Check

A way to solve some problems is to guess the answer, then check it. If it is not right, try again. Use what you learned from the first try to make your next guess better. Guess and check until you find the right answer.

STEP 1 — Read the problem.

NaSha has a total of 10 plastic dinosaurs. She has 6 more green dinosaurs than brown ones. How many of each does she have?

STEP 2 — List the facts.

Fact 1: *NaSha has 10 plastic dinosaurs.*
Fact 2: *She has 6 more green dinosaurs than brown ones.*
Fact 3: *She has at least 6 green plastic dinosaurs.*

STEP 3 — Think about what numbers would give you the answer.

Make a table of your guesses.
Guess 1: $6 + 4 = 10$ **Check:** $6 - 4 = 2$ 6 is only 2 more than 4.
Guess 2: $8 + 2 = 10$ **Check:** $8 - 2 = 6$ 8 is 6 more than 2.
NaSha has 8 green and 2 brown plastic dinosaurs.

Try It!   Use guess and check to solve these problems.

1. Austin's friends made a dinosaur banner for his birthday party. The banner's perimeter is 32 feet. The long sides are 4 feet longer than the short sides. How long is each short side?

_____

2. Jose and 7 friends are playing a dinosaur board game. The game has 19 cards. All players have a Brontosaurus card and a Triceratops card. Some players have a Tyrannosaurus Rex card. If all of the cards are being used, how many players have a Tyrannosaurus Rex card?

_____

Unit 6, Mixed Operations
Problem Solving Strategies 4, SV 0515-4

Name _____ Date _____

STARGAZING

Strategy: Use Estimation

You do not always need an exact answer to solve a problem. You can solve such problems by estimating. To estimate, round each number to the same place. Then choose an operation to solve the problem using the rounded numbers.

STEP 1 **Read the problem.**
Dale watched a movie and went to the observatory at an astronomy museum. The movie lasted 23 minutes. He was in the observatory for 47 minutes. About how long was Dale at the museum?

STEP 2 **List the facts.**
Fact 1: *The movie lasted 23 minutes.*
Fact 2: *He was in the observatory for 47 minutes.*

STEP 3 **Round each number.**
23 → 20   47 → 50

STEP 4 **Add. Solve the problem.**
20 + 50 = 70
Dale spent about 70 minutes at the museum.

Try It! Use estimation to solve these problems.

1. Alex counted 17 stars in an imaginary square in the sky. She estimated that she could see 24 squares in the sky, each with 17 stars. About how many stars could Alex see?

_____

When would Alex use this strategy?

_____

_____

2. Mario counted about 796 stars in the sky. If he filled the sky with 24 imaginary squares all the same size, about how many stars could he see in 1 square?

_____

3. Keiko loves to read about the stars. If she read a total of 277 pages in 4 books, about how many pages are in each book?

_____

Name _____ Date _____

Unit 6 Review

Show What You Know!

Solve each problem. Identify the strategy you used.

1. Lester planted 20 flowers in his garden. He put the flowers in 2 rows. How many flowers did he put in each row? What number sentence would you use to solve this problem?

_____

2. Juanita decorated 137 plastic eggs. Each carton held 12 eggs. About how many cartons did Juanita need for her decorated eggs?

_____

3. Nadia swam 7 laps in the community pool on Wednesday, 6 laps on Thursday, and 7 laps on Friday. How many laps did Nadia swim? How did you figure out the answer?

_____

4. On Saturday, Reese collected at least 10 pounds of plastic to recycle. On Sunday, he collected 8 pounds of plastic to recycle. About how much plastic did he collect in the 2 days?

_____

5. Debbie and Ron invited 10 guests over for pizza. They invited more men than women. There were at least 4 women guests. How many of the guests were men?

_____

Unit 6 Review, page 2

Show What You Know! Complete the table. Solve each problem.

Dirk read a variety of books over the summer. He read 6 mysteries in June, 7 in July, and 9 in August. He read 6 science fiction stories in June, 5 in July, and 3 in August. He read 8 adventure stories in June, 2 in July, and 6 in August.

	June	July	August	Totals
Mysteries				
Science Fiction				
Adventures				
Totals				

1. How many mysteries did Dirk read during the summer? _____

2. How many science fiction stories did Dirk read in the summer? _____

3. How many adventure stories did Dirk read in the summer? _____

4. How many books did Dirk read in June? _____

5. How many books did Dirk read in July? _____

6. How many books did Dirk read in August? _____

Extension ....

Make a table that shows how many minutes you spend each day at school on subjects such as math, reading, spelling, science, and social studies. Write questions about the data in the table. Then use the table to answer your questions.

FLEX YOUR MATH MUSCLES

1

Flex went to a dog show. In the ring he counted 22 heads and 72 feet. How many people and how many dogs were in the ring?

people _____

dogs _____

2

Flex is working a word puzzle. Can you help him guess the missing word?

TAP ➡ PAL ➡ PAT ➡ __ __ __

3

Flex went camping by a river. He needed exactly 9 gallons of water to wash dishes. He had a 6-gallon bucket and a 5-gallon bucket. Using these he measured exactly 9 gallons. How did he do it? (Hint: it helps to draw pictures of the buckets)

_____

_____

_____

_____

4

Flex has been tossing a penny in the air and watching it come down heads or tails. The penny has landed heads up 50 times in a row. What are the chances of the penny landing heads up the next time he tosses the coin?

_____

_____

Name _____ Date _____

WINDOWS TO THE WORLD

Strategy: Define Fractions

A fraction names part of a whole. We read 1/4 or $\frac{1}{4}$, as one fourth.

$$\frac{\text{numerator}}{\text{denominator}} \qquad \frac{1}{4}$$

STEP 1 ▷ **Read the problem.**
Christina is helping with housework. She will wash one fourth of Window A. Shade in the part of the window that Christina will wash.

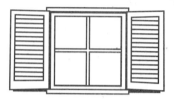
Window A

STEP 2 ▷ **Identify the facts.**
Window A has 4 equal parts.

STEP 3 ▷ **Decide what the problem is asking.**
Shade in $\frac{1}{4}$, or one fourth, of the window.

Window A

STEP 4 ▷ **Solve the problem.**
Shade in 1 square.

Try It! Use fractions to solve these problems.

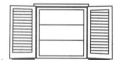
Window B

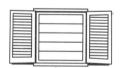
Window C

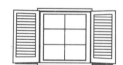
Window D

1. Window B has how many equal parts? _____
   Shade in one third, or $\frac{1}{3}$, of Window B.

2. Christina washes $\frac{3}{5}$ of Window C. How many window panes are not washed? _____
   Shade in the fraction of unwashed window in Window C. What fraction is this? _____

3. If Christina washes $\frac{1}{6}$ of Window D, and her brother washes $\frac{2}{6}$, how much of Window D has been washed?
   _____
   Shade in the fraction of unwashed window in Window D. What fraction is this? _____

Unit 7, Fractions
Problem Solving Strategies 4, SV 0515-4

A RAINBOW WORLD

Strategy: Use Fractions

A fraction names any part of a group. 4 of the 8 pieces of chalk are shaded. $\frac{4}{8}$ is shaded.

You can use fractions to find part of a group. To find $\frac{1}{2}$ of a number, you can divide by 2. $\frac{1}{2}$ of 8, or 4, are shaded.

STEP 1 ⟩ **Read the problem.**
Pablo has 16 crayons. He gives $\frac{1}{4}$ of the crayons to Angie. How many crayons does he give to Angie?

STEP 2 ⟩ **Decide what the problem is asking.**
What is $\frac{1}{4}$ of 16? To find $\frac{1}{4}$ of a number, divide by 4.

STEP 3 ⟩ **Divide. Solve the problem.**
$16 \div 4 = 4$ or $\frac{4}{16}$
Pablo will give Angie 4 crayons.

Try It! Use fractions to solve these problems.

1. Singh has 18 markers. He gives $\frac{1}{6}$ of the markers to his sister. How many markers does he give his sister?

_____

2. Thu has 6 sheets of green paper and 6 sheets of yellow paper. She gives $\frac{1}{3}$ of all her paper to Hoa. How many sheets of paper does she give to Hoa?

_____

3. Mr. Skitt has 20 jars of paint. He gives each group $\frac{1}{5}$ of the paint. How many jars of paint does each group get?

_____

4. Each group of students shares $\frac{1}{4}$ of a box of 24 colored pencils. If each person gets 1 pencil, how many people are in a group?

_____

Name _____ Date _____

IT'S LUNCH TIME!
COME AND GET IT!

Strategy: Make a Drawing

When you read a problem, you might not know at once how to solve it. A drawing helps organize the information in a problem. Be sure you put all the facts in the picture. Sometimes labels help.

STEP 1 ▷ Read the problem.

Diego cut a square sandwich into fourths. He shared the sandwich equally with a friend. How many parts of the sandwich did each person get?

STEP 2 ▷ List the facts.

Fact 1: *Diego and his friend shared a sandwich that was cut into fourths.*
Fact 2: *One sandwich is shared equally.*

STEP 3 ▷ Make a drawing.

STEP 4 ▷ Solve the problem.

From the drawing, you can see that each person gets $\frac{2}{4}$, or $\frac{1}{2}$, of the sandwich.

Try It!   Draw a picture to help solve these problems.

1. Thomasin has a birthday cake to share with 3 friends. If she cuts the cake into 12 equal pieces, what fraction of the cake will each person get?

2. Mr. Horak made a peach cobbler for his family of 4. He cut the cobbler into 8 servings. What fraction of the cobbler can each family member have?

3. Selena is making 6 tacos for her family. She cuts 2 tomatoes. What fraction of a tomato is used in each taco?

Name _____ Date _____

FIELD TRIP!

Strategy: Choose an Operation

Sometimes a problem does not tell you whether to add or subtract. Read the problem carefully. Decide what the problem is asking you to do. Then solve the problem.

STEP 1 **Read the problem.**

Mr. Shepherd's class went to the amusement park. $\frac{9}{23}$ of the class rode the roller coaster. $\frac{6}{23}$ of the class rode the Ferris wheel. How much more of the class rode the roller coaster than rode the Ferris wheel? What fraction of the class rode neither the roller coaster nor the Ferris wheel?

STEP 2 **Decide what the problem is asking.**

How much more of the class rode the roller coaster than rode the Ferris wheel? What fraction of the class rode neither the roller coaster nor the Ferris wheel?

STEP 3 **Choose an operation.**

To find how many more rode the roller coaster, you must subtract. To find the fraction of students who didn't go on either ride, first find what fraction did ride. Then subtract from the whole to find the difference.

STEP 4 **Subtract. Solve the problem.**

A. $\frac{9}{23} - \frac{6}{23} = \frac{3}{23}$ **B.** $\frac{9}{23} + \frac{6}{23} = \frac{15}{23}$ $\frac{23}{23} - \frac{15}{23} = \frac{8}{23}$

A. $\frac{3}{23}$ more of the class rode the roller coaster than the Ferris wheel.

B. $\frac{8}{23}$ of the class rode neither ride.

Try It! Choose an operation to solve the problem.

1. Of the students who wanted to ride the tilt-a-whirl, $\frac{11}{17}$ were tall enough. What fraction of the students were not tall enough?

_____

Name _____ Date _____

OFF TO ENGLAND!

Strategy: Add Mixed Numbers

Whether adding or subtracting mixed numbers, add or subtract the fractions first, then do the whole numbers.

STEP 1 ▷ Read the problem.
Mr. and Mrs. O'Cleary are taking their 3 children on a vacation trip. The airline trip from their hometown to Chicago is $1{,}615\frac{4}{10}$ miles. Where could their hometown be? From Chicago they will fly to England, which is $4{,}025\frac{5}{10}$ miles. How many miles will they fly?

STEP 2 ▷ Decide what the problem is asking.
Where could their hometown be? How many miles will they fly altogether?
Use an atlas to research towns that are 1,615 miles from Chicago!

STEP 3 ▷ Choose an operation.
Altogether signals addition.

STEP 4 ▷ Add. Solve the problem.

$$1{,}615\frac{4}{10} \text{ miles}$$
$$+\ 4{,}025\frac{5}{10} \text{ miles}$$
$$\overline{5{,}640\frac{9}{10} \text{ miles}}$$

The O'Cleary family will fly $5{,}640\frac{9}{10}$ miles.

Try It! Choose an operation to solve the problems.

1. The family took a bus $53\frac{1}{5}$ miles to the English coast. Then they took a ferry $30\frac{3}{5}$ miles across the water to reach Ireland. How far did they travel?

_____

About how many total miles have they traveled for this trip?

_____

2. Colin went to visit an old castle. He walked $1\frac{4}{6}$ miles to the castle and $1\frac{1}{6}$ miles inside the castle. Then he walked back to the hotel. How far did he walk?

_____

Name _____ Date _____

FUEL UP

Strategy: Subtract Mixed Numbers

When adding or subtracting mixed numbers, add or subtract the fractions first, then the whole numbers.

 Read the problem.

Mrs. Rzepka's gas gauge showed that she had used $7\frac{9}{10}$ gallons of gas. She wanted to start on a trip with a full tank of gas. However, she had only enough money to buy $6\frac{7}{10}$ gallons. How much less gas did she buy than she needed for a full tank?

 Decide what the problem is asking.

How much less gas did she buy?

 Choose an operation.

To find the difference, you must subtract.

STEP 4 Solve the problem.

$$\begin{array}{r} 7\frac{9}{10} \\ -\ 6\frac{7}{10} \\ \hline 1\frac{2}{10} \end{array}$$

Mrs. Rzepka bought $1\frac{2}{10}$ fewer gallons than she needed for a full tank.

Try It! Choose an operation to solve the problems.

1. Ramie is making a cake. She needs $4\frac{3}{4}$ cups of flour, but she only has $3\frac{1}{4}$. How much flour does she need to borrow?

_____

If she borrows 2 cups, will she have enough?

_____

How much more or less will that be?

_____

2. Deanna has $6\frac{4}{12}$ oz of cat food. If she feeds her cat $2\frac{2}{12}$ oz for lunch, how much cat food will she have left?

_____

Does she have enough to feed her cat this amount for 2 more days?

_____

Problem Solving Strategies 4, SV 0515-4

FIXING UP THE HOUSE

Strategy: Choose an Operation

When adding or subtracting mixed numbers, add or subtract the fractions first, then the whole numbers. In 2-step problems, you may have to use more than 1 operation.

 Read the problem.

Danielle is fixing the stairs. She has a piece of wood $8\frac{9}{12}$ ft long. She needs a $4\frac{6}{12}$ ft board and a $3\frac{3}{12}$ ft board. How much wood will she have left after she fixes the stairs?

 Decide what the problem is asking.

How much wood will be left?

STEP 3 **List the facts.**

Fact 1: *Danielle has a board $8\frac{9}{12}$ ft long.*

Fact 2: *She needs a $4\frac{6}{12}$ ft board.*

Fact 3: *She needs a $3\frac{3}{12}$ ft board.*

STEP 4 **Choose an operation.**

To find the sum, add. To find the difference, subtract.

STEP 5 **Add and subtract. Solve the problem.**

Step 1:
$$4\frac{6}{12}\text{ ft}$$
$$+\ 3\frac{3}{12}\text{ ft}$$
$$\overline{7\frac{9}{12}\text{ ft}}$$

Step 2:
$$8\frac{9}{12}\text{ ft}$$
$$-\ 7\frac{9}{12}\text{ ft}$$
$$\overline{1\text{ ft}}$$

Danielle will have 1 foot of wood left.

Try It! Choose an operation to solve the problems.

1. Stefan put in new countertops. The countertops were the following lengths: $2\frac{5}{12}$ ft, $2\frac{2}{12}$ ft, $2\frac{4}{12}$ ft. How many feet of countertop were there?'

_____

2. If Stefan started with a board 8 ft long, how much would he have left?

_____

What else could he build?

_____

Name _____ Date _____

Unit 7 Review

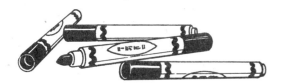

Show What You Know!

Solve each problem. Identify the strategy you used.

1. Greg has a box of 12 markers. He pulls $\frac{1}{4}$ of the markers out of the box. How many markers did he pull out of the box?

_____

2. LaToya made a design with 8 triangles. She colored 4 of them red. Draw a picture that shows the fraction of triangles that LaToya colored red.

_____

3. Gregor needed to put his toys away. He put $\frac{1}{3}$ of his toys on shelves in his closet and $\frac{1}{3}$ in a large box. What fraction of his toys did Gregor put away? What fraction of his toys did Gregor still need to put away?

_____

4. Shade the circle to show the fraction $\frac{3}{8}$.

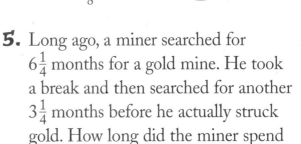

5. Long ago, a miner searched for $6\frac{1}{4}$ months for a gold mine. He took a break and then searched for another $3\frac{1}{4}$ months before he actually struck gold. How long did the miner spend searching before he struck gold?

_____

6. The miner found $2\frac{3}{8}$ ounces of gold. He used $1\frac{1}{8}$ ounces to buy some supplies. How much gold did he have left?

_____

Unit 7 Review, page 2

Show What You Know!

Solve each problem. Identify the strategy you used.

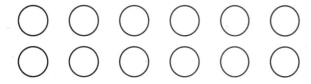

1. Shade the circles to show the fraction $\frac{9}{12}$.

_____

2. Evan wanted to make Valentine's Day cards for the 23 students in his class. He has already made 12 of the cards. What fraction tells how many cards he has already made? What fraction tells how many cards he still needs to make?

_____

3. Jade made 12 cookies for her 3 friends. She gave each friend the same number of cookies. Draw a picture to show what fraction of the cookies one friend got.

4. In June, the town of Marble Falls got $9\frac{4}{16}$ inches of rain. In July, the town got $12\frac{7}{16}$ inches of rain. How much rain did Marble Falls get during the 2 months?

_____

5. Mrs. Nagel bought a package of 50 gold stars for her students. She has already used $\frac{1}{2}$ of the stars. How many stars did Mrs. Nagel use?

_____

6. Frederica had $50\frac{17}{20}$ pounds of oats for her horses. She used $22\frac{2}{20}$ pounds. How many pounds of oats does she have left?

_____

Name _____ Date _____

FLEX YOUR MATH MUSCLES

You can have a lot of fun with fractions.

1

Divide 30 by $\frac{1}{2}$ and add 10. What is your answer?

_____

2

Pablo and Flex are driving in a 200-mile race. Pablo can complete 1 lap in 4 minutes. It takes Flex $\frac{1}{2}$ the time it takes Pablo to complete a lap. How many more laps does Flex make in 1 hour than Pablo does?

_____

3

Flex went shopping in 5 stores. He had $1.50 left when he finished shopping. In each store, he spent half of what he had when he entered the store. How much money did Flex have when he started his shopping spree? (Hint: Work backward. Flex had $1.50 when he finished.)

_____

4

On a shopping trip, 2 mothers and 2 daughters each bought a dress. They spent a total of $75. Each one spent $\frac{1}{3}$ of the total. How much did each one spend?

_____

How could 2 mothers and 2 daughters each spend $\frac{1}{3}$ of the total?

_____

Name _____ Date _____

PENNY WISE

Strategy: Change Money

penny	nickel	dime	quarter	half dollar
1¢ or $0.01	5¢ or $0.05	10¢ or $0.10	25¢ or $0.25	50¢ or $0.50

1-dollar bill   5-dollar bill   10-dollar bill

Use a decimal to separate the number of dollars from the number of cents:

two dollars and eighty-one cents = $2.81

Try It! (Remember that 1 dollar = 100 cents.)

1. How many dimes do you need to make 1 dollar?

_____

2. A dime is what fraction of 1 dollar?

_____

3. How many quarters do you need to make 1 dollar?

_____

4. A quarter is what fraction of 1 dollar?

_____

5. How many nickels do you need to make fifty cents? _____

How many quarters?

_____

6. A nickel is what fraction of a dime?

_____

7. What is the value of 4 dimes and 2 nickels?

_____

8. What is the value of 1 quarter, 1 dime, 1 nickel, and 1 penny?

_____

9. Three dollars and twenty cents =

$ _____ . _____

10. Seven cents   =

$ _____ . _____

Unit 8, Decimals and Money
Problem Solving Strategies 4, SV 0515-4

WE ALL SCREAM FOR ICE CREAM!

Strategy: Add Money

When adding or subtracting money, line up the decimal points. Then line up the digits on each side of the decimal points.

 Read the problem.

Kim wants to buy a chocolate sundae for $3.20. Toppings are $0.55 extra. She wants nuts for her topping. How much money does Kim need?

 Line up the decimal points and the digits on each side of the decimal points.

$$\begin{array}{r} \$3.20 \\ + \ \$0.55 \\ \hline ? \end{array}$$

STEP 3 **Add. Solve the problem.**

Add. Write your answer in dollars and cents.

$$\begin{array}{r} \$3.20 \\ + \ \$0.55 \\ \hline \$3.75 \end{array} \qquad \text{Kim needs } \$3.75$$

Try It! Write the numbers in dollars and cents, then add to find the answers.

1. Marie wants to buy an ice cream cone for $1.20. She has 3 quarters, 2 dimes, and 7 pennies. Does she have enough money?

_____

How much money does she have?

_____

2. Pauline and Pierre shared a soda and a banana split. One of them bought the soda for $1.87, and the other bought the ice cream for $5.52. How much did they spend altogether?

_____

Name _____   Date _____

WINTER FUN

Strategy: Subtract Money

When adding or subtracting money, line up the decimal points. Then line up the digits on each side of the decimal points.

 Read the problem.
Dwayne wants to tie-dye a winter jacket. He has $37.25. The jacket costs $28.50. How much does he have left to spend on the dye?

STEP 2 **Line up the decimal points and the digits on each side of the decimal points.**

$$
\begin{array}{r}
\$37.25 \\
-\ \$28.50 \\
\hline
? \\
\end{array}
$$

STEP 3 **Subtract. Solve the problem.**
Subtract. Write your answer in dollars and cents.

$$
\begin{array}{r}
\$37.25 \\
-\ \$28.50 \\
\hline
\$\ 8.75 \\
\end{array}
$$
Dwayne will have $8.75 left.

Try It! Write these problems as money, then subtract to find the answers.

1. Sayad bought a green scarf and a yellow scarf. The green one was $2.25, and the yellow one was $3.75. How much more did he spend on the yellow scarf than on the green scarf?

_____

He gave the clerk $8.00. How much change did he get?

_____

2. Jeremiah needs 2 pairs of mittens to play in the snow. Each pair costs $5.90. Jeremiah has $9.78. How much more money does Jeremiah need to buy mittens?

_____

3. Shing and Hector bought materials to use on their snowman. Shing bought a hat for $2.35 and buttons for $1.18. Hector bought a scarf for $3.50. Who spent more on materials?

_____

Name _____ Date _____

TAKING A TRIP

Strategy: Multiply Money

When multiplying or dividing money, set up your problem like any other multiplication or division problem, but include the dollar sign and decimal point. Write your answer in dollars and cents.

 Read the problem.

Cathy went on vacation. She sent 5 postcards to her friends. If the postcards were 25¢ each, how much money did she spend in all?

STEP 2 Set up the problem.

$$\begin{array}{r} \$0.25 \\ \times \quad 5 \\ \hline ? \end{array}$$

STEP 3 Multiply. Solve the problem.

Multiply. Write your answer in dollars and cents.

$$\begin{array}{r} \$0.25 \\ \times \quad 5 \\ \hline \$1.25 \end{array}$$ Cathy spent $1.25.

Try It! Write these problems as money, then multiply to find the answers.

1. Isabel bought souvenirs for 5 friends from all the places she went on her vacation. She bought 2 T-shirts in Texas for $10.20 each. She bought 3 necklaces in New Orleans for $9.09 each. How much did she spend in all on souvenirs?

_____

2. The Altobelli family went to an amusement park in Florida. Park admission was $15.00 a day for each person. There are 4 people in the Altobelli family. If they went to the park for 3 days, how much did they spend on park admission in all?

_____

Name _____ Date _____

TEAM NEWS

Strategy: Divide Money

When multiplying or dividing money, set up your problem like any other multiplication or division problem, but include the dollar sign and decimal point. Write your answer in dollars and cents.

 Read the problem.

There are 4 girls on the volleyball team who need new uniforms. These uniforms cost a total of $70. How much will each girl pay?

 Set up the problem.

$$4\overline{)\$70.00}\overset{?}{}$$

STEP 3 **Divide. Solve the problem.**

$$\overset{\$17.50}{4\overline{)\$70.00}}$$ Each girl will pay $17.50

Try It!

Write these problems as money, then divide to find the answers. (Hint: Some problems have two steps.)

1. The science club is going to a state competition. It will cost $750 for the club to travel to the state capital. There are 14 club members and a coach. If they share the cost equally, how much will each person pay?

_____

2. The drama club bought 40 props for a play. Each prop cost $3.50. They have to charge admission to the play in order to pay for the props. If 20 people come to the show, how much should they charge each person?

_____

3. The school band needs 10 music stands. The music stands cost a total of $184.50. How much does each one cost?

_____

4. Your school is selling spirit T-shirts to raise money for new basketball uniforms. The T-shirts cost $5.00 each. The school needs to raise $900 to buy 45 new uniforms. How many T-shirts do they need to sell to pay for the uniforms?

_____

Name _____ Date _____

TIME TO BUY LUNCH!

Strategy: Guess and Check

A good way to solve some problems is to guess the answer, then check it. If your guess is not right, try again. Use what you learned from the first try to make your next guess better. Guess and check until you find the answer.

STEP 1 ▸ **Read the problem.**
Deidre spent 65¢ on fruit. What kinds of fruit did she buy?

STEP 2 ▸ **Guess.**
A banana and an apple.

MENU

muffin	65¢	milk	30¢	banana	30¢
bagel	45¢	juice box	25¢	apple	35¢
cookie	35¢	soda pop	50¢	orange	40¢

STEP 3 ▸ **Check.**
30¢ + 35¢ = 65¢ Deidre bought a banana and an apple.
If your guess is incorrect, guess again and check your new answer.

 Try It! Look at the menu to solve each problem. Guess and check to find the answers.

1. Anita spent 35¢ more than Donna. Donna spent 55¢. How much did Anita spend?

   _____

   What might Donna have bought?

   _____

2. Arwen bought a soda. He wants to buy a pastry. If he started with $1.05, which pastry could he buy?

   _____ or _____

   How much money would he have left?

   _____

3. Noel bought 2 pieces of the same fruit. Then he bought a juice box. He spent 85¢. Which fruit did he buy?

   _____

4. Mariko is buying a snack for herself and 2 friends. She has $1.80. She wants milk, and each of her friends wants a juice box. If all 3 girls eat something, what can they buy?

   _____

   _____

Name _____ Date _____

HAPPY BIRTHDAY, MOM!

Strategy: Identify Extra or Missing Information

Some problems may give too many facts. Other problems may not give enough facts. Read the problem carefully. If there is too much information, cross out the extra facts. Then solve the problem. If there is not enough information, decide what information is still needed.

STEP 1 ▷ **Read the problem.**

Jenine went shopping for her mom's birthday. She bought roses for $15 and a vase for $5. Jenine had $23. Does she have enough money left to buy a birthday card?

STEP 2 ▷ **Decide what the problem is asking.**

Does she have enough money left to buy a card?

STEP 3 ▷ **Identify the facts.**

Fact 1: *She bought roses for $15 and a vase for $5.*
Fact 2: *Jenine had $23.*

STEP 4 ▷ **Identify extra or missing facts.**

Missing fact: How much does the birthday card cost?

STEP 5 ▷ **Solve the problem.**

There is not enough information to solve this problem.

Try It! Identify the extra or missing facts in these problems.

1. At Mama's Cafe, Jenine's dad bought dinner for the family. There are 4 people in their family. He spent $12.50 on each person. How much change did he get?

_____

Extra or Missing Facts?

_____

2. It costs $7.75 for a birthday cake. It costs $6.00 to have "Happy Birthday" on the cake. Candles are $2.00. Jenine gave the baker $15.00. How much change did she get?

_____

Extra or Missing Facts?

_____

Problem Solving Strategies 4, SV 0515-4

Name _____ Date _____

Unit 8 Review

Show What You Know!

Solve each problem. Identify the strategy you used.

1. How many quarters make 1 dollar?

_____

2. Over the weekend, Darcy did some extra chores around the house. On Saturday, she earned $3.25. On Sunday, she earned $5.25. How much money did she earn altogether?

_____

3. There were 6 workers at a construction site. They each spent $3.25 to buy a lunch. What is the total amount that the 6 workers spent on their lunches?

_____

4. A penny is what fraction of a dollar?

_____

5. The fourth-graders at Flannigan Elementary School put on a carnival. They earned $366.05. An equal amount of that money was given to each of the 5 fourth-grade teachers to buy books for their students. How much did each teacher get?

_____

6. A quarter is what fraction of a dollar?

_____

Unit 8 Review, page 2

Strategies

- Change Money
- Add Money
- Subtract Money
- Multiply Money
- Divide Money
- Guess and Check
- Identify Extra or Missing Information

Show What You Know!

Solve each problem. Identify the strategy you used.

1. Denise invited 12 friends to her party. She bought party favors for $23.45. How much change did she get?

_____

2. Mr. and Mrs. Hoover bought movie tickets. The tickets for children cost $2.00. The tickets for adults cost $3.00. They spent a total of $10.00. How many adult and children's tickets did the Hoovers buy?

_____

3. How many nickels do you need to make 1 dollar?

_____

4. Mr. Tomlinson took a check for $65.23 to his bank. He asked the cashier for $25.50 in cash and told her to deposit the rest in his account. How much money did Mr. Tomlinson deposit in his bank account?

_____

5. What is the value of 2 quarters, 2 dimes, and 2 pennies?

_____

6. Quentin went to a garage sale at Mrs. Jones' house. He bought a video game for $7.30 at the sale. He gave Mrs. Jones $10. When he got home he played the game for 2 hours. How much change did he get when he bought the game?

_____

Name _____ Date _____

FLEX YOUR MATH MUSCLES

1

Flex bought a hat and a coat. He spent $110. The coat cost $100 more than the hat. How much did the hat cost?

_____

2

Here's a deal for you. On November 1, you ask your mom for an allowance to buy holiday presents. She offers you 2 choices: She will give you $1 each day of the month, OR she will give you a penny on the first day of November, and double the amount she gives each day of the month. If you take the dollar-a-day deal, how much money will you have at the end of the month?

_____

Which of your mom's offers is the better deal?

_____

3

Your uncle has his choice of two good jobs. One job pays $40,000 for his first year of work, with a raise of $8,000 every year after that for 6 years. The other job will pay him $20,000 for his first 6 months of work with a raise of $2,000 every 6 months after that for 6 years. Which job offers a better deal?

_____

4

If you have five apples and eat all but three, how many do you have left? Can you do it? Sure you can!

_____

Name _____ Date _____

MEASURING IT OUT!

Strategy: Work with Standard Units

Measuring is done many ways. Three ways are length, weight, and volume.

The most commonly used measurements for length:	The most commonly used measurements for weight:	The most commonly used measurements for volume:
1 inch (in.) = |————| 1 foot (ft) = 12 inches (in.) 1 yard (yd) = 3 feet (ft) 1 mile = 5,280 feet (ft)	1 ounce (oz) = about the weight of 1 slice of bread 1 pound (lb) = 16 oz 1 ton (T) = 2,000 lb	1 cup (c) = school milk carton 1 pint (pt) = 2 c 1 quart (qt) = 2 pt 1 gallon (g) = 4 qt

We usually use only one type of measurement for a given object. For example, if you wanted to know how much you had grown over the past year, you would measure your length, or height, in feet and inches. If you were carrying a bucket of sand, you might like to know its weight in pounds. When measuring liquids for cooking, you use volume, or capacity, usually by the cup.

Which measurement would you use to tell the height of a flagpole?

_____

Which measurement would you use to tell the weight of the flagpole?

_____

Try It! For each of the following examples, write 2 units of measurement for each item. The first example is done for you.

	Length	Weight	Volume
1. Your body	inches	pounds	would not use
2. A candle			
3. A thermos full of milk			
4. A truck full of gravel			
5. A juice box			

Name _____ Date _____

THINKING METRIC

Strategy: Work with Metric Units

The metric system is a system of measurement based on units of 10. Most of the world uses the metric system as its standard. The United States is the only nation that does not commonly use the metric system.

The most common metric units used to measure length are:

1 meter (m) = about 39 in. (3 inches longer than a yard stick)

1 centimeter (cm) = $\frac{1}{100}$ m; there are 100 cm in 1 m

STEP 1 ▷ **Read the problem.**
Estephan and Bryce are using wire for their science project. They cut a piece of wire 200 cm long. How many meters of wire do they use?

STEP 2 ▷ **Identify the facts.**
They cut a piece of wire 200 cm long.

STEP 3 ▷ **Decide what the problem is asking.**
How many meters of wire do they use?

STEP 4 ▷ **Choose the operation.**
To change cm to m, you must divide by 100.

STEP 5 ▷ **Divide. Solve the problem.**
200 cm ÷ 100 = 2 m

Try It! Solve the problems.

1. Josh and Mary Ann need 4 m of string for their science project. How many cm will they use?

_____

2. Naka measured the length of the science classroom at 21 m. How many cm did he measure?

_____

Name _____ Date _____

WEIGH OUT!

Strategy: Use Metric Weight

The most common metric units used to measure weight, or mass, are:

1 gram (g) = about the weight of a small paper clip
1 kilogram (kg) = 1,000 g

STEP 1 ▸ **Read the problem.**
The project that Jeffrey and Gordon are doing needs 7 kg of sand. How many grams of sand do they need?

STEP 2 ▸ **Identify the facts.**
They need 7 kg of sand.

STEP 3 ▸ **Decide what the problem is asking.**
How many grams of sand do they need?

STEP 4 ▸ **Choose the operation.**
To change kg to g, you must multiply by 1,000.

STEP 5 ▸ **Multiply. Solve the problem.**
7 kg × 1,000 = 7,000 g

Try It! Solve the problems.

1. Manny and Serena have a science project that is full of rocks. It weighs 10,000 g! What is this weight in kg?

_____

2. Josefina has just received a present for her birthday. It weighs 5,000 g. How many kg does the present weigh?

_____

3. Warren's cat weighs 4 kg. Leesha's cat weighs 5 kg. How many g do their cats weigh in all?

_____

4. Hannah weighs 21 kg. Her brother weighs 18 kg. How many more g does Hannah weigh than her brother?

_____

Problem Solving Strategies 4, SV 0515-4

Name _____ Date _____

POURING IT ON!

Strategy: Measure Liquids

The most common metric units used to measure volume, or capacity, are:

liter (L) = approximately the size of 1 quart

milliliter (mL) = $\frac{1}{1,000}$ of a liter; there are 1,000 mL in a L

STEP 1 ▷ Read the problem.
Juanita and Raoul have spilled 1 L of the rain water they had collected for their project! They started with 4 L of water. How many more mL of rain water do they have to collect to replace the spilled water?

STEP 2 ▷ Identify the facts.
Fact 1: *They started with 4 L of water.*
Fact 2: *They spilled 1 L of the water.*

STEP 3 ▷ Decide what the problem is asking.
In this problem, "How many more mL?" is the question.

STEP 4 ▷ Choose the operation.
To change L to mL, you must multiply by 1,000.

STEP 5 ▷ Multiply. Solve the problem.
1 L × 1,000 = 1,000 mL

Try It! Solve the problems.

1. James and Tanya have used $\frac{1}{2}$ bottle of vinegar in their project. The bottle holds 1 L of vinegar. How many mL of vinegar do they have left?

_____

2. DeLinda and Jesse filled each of 2 beakers with 1,000 mL of oil. They decided to use only 1 beaker for their project. How many L of oil did they use?

_____

HOW DO YOU MEASURE UP?

Strategy: Choose a Measurement

Try It! Choose 2 types of metric measurement that make sense for each example. Use *cm, m, g, kg, mL,* or *L.*

1. your finger _____

2. a juice box _____

3. an elephant _____

4. you _____

5. a highway _____

6. an ant _____

7. your desk _____

8. an eyedropper _____

9. a classroom _____

10. a baby bottle _____

11. a milk truck _____

12. an airplane _____

13. a swimming pool _____

14. a water tower _____

15. a train engine _____

16. a glass of soda _____

17. a mouse _____

18. a chalkboard _____

19. a bathtub _____

20. a brick _____

Name _____ Date _____

HEATING IT UP!

Strategy: Measure Temperature

The metric system has a different scale of measuring heat, too. In the United States, we use the Fahrenheit (F) scale. Water freezes at 32° F and boils at 212° F. Using the metric Celsius (C) scale, water freezes at 0° C and boils at 100° C.

Try It! Follow the directions to solve each problem.

1. What is the Celsius temperature at which the ice in your freezer will be ready for you to use?

   _____

2. What is the Celsius temperature at which you can boil your eggs for breakfast?

   _____

3. If 0° C is freezing and 100° C is boiling, at about what temperature would the lake be good for swimming?

   _____

4. Where you live, about what temperature is it in September?

   _____

5. If you were going sledding, it would be about what temperature?

   _____

6. What are some of the clothes you would wear outside on a day that was 2° C?

   _____

   _____

   _____

7. What kind of activity would be good for you and your friends to do on a day when the thermometer reads 33° C?

   _____

   _____

8. Where do you probably live if it's 33° C in March?

   _____

Name _____ Date _____

WATCHING THE CLOCK

Strategy: Measure Time

Clocks show hours, minutes, and sometimes seconds.
Both of these clocks show the same time:

40 minutes after 3, or 3:40

| 1 minute = 60 seconds | 1 hour = 60 minutes | 1 day = 24 hours |

Try It! Follow the directions to solve each problem.

1. Write the time shown on each clock.

_____   _____   _____

2. Draw the hour hand and the minute hand to show each time.

3:05   4:35   10:00

12:30   8:15

Write the answers to the following questions:

3. How many minutes are in 1 day?

_____

4. How many seconds are in 1 hour?

_____

5. Activity: Using a clock with a second hand and a partner who can watch it for you, close your eyes and see if you can guess when 1 minute has passed. Watch the clock for your partner. Was a minute longer or shorter than you thought it would be?

_____

Unit 9, Measurement
Problem Solving Strategies 4, SV 0515-4

Unit 9 Review

Show What You Know!

Solve each problem. Identify the strategy you used.

---

1. Veronica bought 2 liters of oil for her father's car. How many milliliters of oil did she buy?

_____

_____

2. What are some clothes you might wear outside if it is 95° F?

_____

_____

3. Draw the hour hand and the minute hand to show 6:50 on the clock.

_____

4. Preston spent 120 minutes practicing the guitar. How many hours did he spend practicing?

_____

_____

5. Which 2 units of measure could you use for a dog? Circle your answers.

length   weight   volume

_____

6. If a thermometer reads 32° F, what is the temperature in degrees Celsius?

_____

_____

Show What You Know!

Solve each problem. Identify the strategy you used.

1. What 2 types of metric measurement could you use to measure the length of a kite string? (Use the abbreviations *cm, m, g, kg, mL,* or *L.*)

   _____

2. Which measure would you use to find the length of a river?

   _____

3. How many centimeters are in 3 meters?

   _____

4. Which 2 units of measure could you use for a container of gasoline? Circle your answers.

   length   weight   volume

5. Daryl received a package that weighed 3 kilograms. How many grams did the package weigh?

   _____

6. What 2 types of metric measurement could you use to measure the amount of water in a plastic jug?

   _____

Extension

Look up a simple recipe in a cookbook. Determine how much of each ingredient you would need if you doubled the recipe.

FLEX YOUR MATH MUSCLES

1

Flex is having some fun on his day off. He woke up at 7:30 in the morning. It took him 45 minutes to get to the lake and 45 minutes to get home. He spent 5 hours at the lake and 2 hours shopping for antiques. What time did Flex get home?

_____

3

On Flex's way home, he stops at some antique stores. The first store is 6 miles from the lake. The second store is 12 miles from the first store. The last store is just 1 mile from Flex's house. If the second store is 3 miles away from Flex's house, how far is the lake from Flex's house?

_____

2

On Flex's day off, he is driving his boat around his favorite lake. Flex makes 3 trips around the lake. It takes him $1\frac{1}{2}$ hours to go all the way around the lake on each of his first 2 trips. His third trip takes him 1 hour and 30 minutes. Why?

_____

4

Flex was thirsty when he got home! He drank 1 quart of water. He was still thirsty, so he drank 2 cups of juice. Then with dinner, he drank a pint of milk and a cup of tea. How many cups of liquid did Flex drink altogether?

_____

Name _____ Date _____

THINK IT THROUGH

Strategy: Make a Table

If a problem is tricky, use logic to solve the problem. Using logic is thinking carefully about each clue. First read the problem. Then look for clues. Make a table to keep track of clues. Use the clues to solve the problem.

STEP 1 ▷ Read the problem.

Ricky and Lucy both have soccer balls. One ball is white, and the other one is yellow. Lucy says they have to play with Ricky's soccer ball because her white one is flat. Who has the yellow ball?

STEP 2 ▷ Look for clues.

Lucy's white ball is flat.

STEP 3 ▷ Make a table.

Fill in the table using the clues.

	white	yellow
Ricky		
Lucy	YES	

STEP 4 ▷ Fill in the table. Solve the problem.

If there is a YES either across or down, the other spaces in that row or column have a NO in them.

	white	yellow
Ricky	NO	YES
Lucy	YES	NO

Ricky has the yellow ball.

USE LOGIC TO SOLVE PROBLEMS

Strategy: Look for Clues

Try It! Fill in the tables to solve the problems.

1. Linda and Julio each eat a piece of pizza. One pizza is pepperoni, and one is cheese. Linda will not eat the cheese pizza. Who will eat the cheese pizza?

	pepperoni	cheese
Linda		
Julio		

_____

2. Ryan, Wanda, and Sai each read a book. There was a mystery book, a biography, and a book of riddles. Wanda read the first chapter of the biography. Sai didn't read the mystery. Who read which book?

	mystery	biography	riddles
Ryan			
Wanda			
Sai			

3. Angelo, Wayne, and Adrienne each play a sport. One is a right-handed baseball player. One plays basketball. One plays soccer. Adrienne uses only her feet. Wayne is left-handed. What sport does each one play?

	baseball	basketball	soccer
Angelo			
Wayne			
Adrienne			

4. Erica and James both play video games. One of them had $2, and the other had 6 quarters. Each game costs 25¢. Erica played 8 games. Who had $2, and who had 6 quarters?

	$2	6 quarters
Erica		
James		

_____

Name _____ Date _____

LOOK FOR THE CLUES

Strategy: Make a Table

Sometimes a problem doesn't seem to give enough clues. But you can use logic to solve problems with only 1 or 2 clues.

STEP 1 > Read the problem.

Miss Brown, Mr. Green, and Miss Black are friends. They drive cars that match their names. Miss Brown and the friend with the green car were talking about it:

"Our cars match each of our names, but none of us drives a car of the color that matches our own name," said the friend who drove the green car. What color is each person's car?

STEP 2 > Make a table, and fill in the table from the clues.

Clue 1: *Miss Brown does not have a brown car.*

Clue 2: *Mr. Green does not have a green car.*

Clue 3: *Miss Black does not have a black car.*

Clue 4: *Miss Brown does not have a green car because she was talking to the friend who drove a green car.*

	brown	green	black
Miss Brown	NO	NO	
Mr. Green		NO	
Miss Black			NO

STEP 3 > Fill in the table. Solve the problem.

If there are 2 NOs in a row or column, then the other space has to be YES. When there is a YES in one space, the other 2 spaces in the row or column are NO.

	brown	green	black
Miss Brown	NO	NO	YES
Mr. Green	YES	NO	NO
Miss Black	NO	YES	NO

Miss Brown drives the BLACK car. Mr. Green drives the BROWN car. Miss Black drives the GREEN car.

Problem Solving Strategies 4, SV 0515-4

ELEMENTARY, MY DEAR WATSON!

Strategy: Use Logical Reasoning

Sherlock Holmes was a great detective in mystery stories. He used logic to solve mysteries. He often said to his assistant, Dr. Watson, "Elementary, my dear Watson." Use logic to solve these problems.

Try It! Fill in the tables. Write YES or NO in the boxes to solve the problems.

1. Kim, Dee, and Paul surfed the Internet using a home computer, a school computer, and a laptop computer. Dee did not use a home computer. Paul carries his computer with him. Who used which computer?

	home computer	school computer	laptop computer
Kim			
Dee			
Paul			

2. Steve, Jesse, and Karim went on vacation. One went river-rafting, one went rock-climbing, and one went surfing. Steve took a canoe and paddle. Karim went in a swimsuit. Who did what?

	river-rafting	rock-climbing	surfing
Steve			
Jesse			
Karim			

3. Kendra, Nadia, and Brett each began a test at the same time. One finished at 9:00, one at 10:00, and one at 11:00 in the morning. Brett took the most time to finish. Kendra did not finish first. Who finished at which time? Finish the table to solve the problem.

		10:00	
Kendra			

Name _____ Date _____

WHO'S WHO AND WHAT'S WHAT

Strategy: Use Logical Reasoning

Filling in a table helps organize your thinking.

Try It! Use tables to solve these problems.

1. Debbie, Dave, and Donna are triplets. One has blonde hair, one has red hair, and one has brown hair. Debbie does not have red hair. The boy has dark hair. Which person has what color hair?

	blonde	red	brown
Debbie			
Dave			
Donna			

2. Mr. Jackson, Miss Morales, and Mrs. O'Hara work at Pine Valley School. One is the principal, one is a kindergarten teacher, and one is a gym teacher. Mr. Jackson told the principal that Miss Morales would be late to the meeting. The kindergarten teacher drives Miss Morales to school every morning.

Which person holds which job?

	principal	kindergarten teacher	gym teacher
Mr. Jackson			
Miss Morales			
Mrs. O'Hara			

Unit 10, Logic
Problem Solving Strategies 4, SV 0515-4

Name _____ Date _____

WELCOME TO YOOHOO

Strategy: Identify True or False

You can solve some logic problems
by knowing whether statements
are true or false.

Read the problem. Can you solve it?

Adam the astronaut is exploring the planet Yoohoo. There are 2 nations on Yoohoo—the States of Yoo and the Kingdom of Hoo. Adam knows that the people of Yoo are friendly, but they talk in code. If he gets to Yoo City, they'll give him yoo-burgers and yoo-cola.

The people of Hoo are unfriendly, and they say the opposite of what they mean. They do this so people will not come to their town. If he goes to Hoo Town, the Hoos will give him worms to eat.

He rides his space bike until he gets to a fork in the road. One fork leads to Yoo City, and the other fork leads to Hoo Town. The sign post is missing, so he doesn't know which fork leads to Yoo City.

A native of Yoohoo is standing at the side of the road. Adam doesn't know if the native is a Yoo or a Hoo.

"How do you get to your hometown?" asks Adam. The YooHoo points to the right fork.

Adam goes in the direction the native is pointing. Why?

Solution: If the native is a Yoo, his code is pointing to Yoo City. If the native is a Hoo, he is saying the opposite of what he means. A Hoo would not point to Hoo Town, but to Yoo City. So Adam should go the direction the native points, whether he is a Yoo or Hoo.

Try It! Use logic to solve the problem.

Adam arrived safely in Yoo City. He asked the first Yoo he saw, "Are you the president of the Yoos?" The Yoo patted his head. Adam wasn't quite sure what that meant, but by asking 1 more question, he figured it out. What did he ask?

_____

Unit 10 Review

Show What You Know!

Solve each problem. Identify the strategy you used.

1. Esther and Hector both have friendship bracelets. One bracelet is blue, and the other is red. Esther's bracelet is broken, so Hector let her borrow the red one. Use a table to keep track of the clues. What color was Esther's bracelet?

	Blue Bracelet	Red Bracelet
Esther		
Hector		

_____

2. The Francisco family, the Landrum family, and the Williams family each adopted a cat from the local animal shelter. The cats that got adopted were a short-haired brown tabby, a long-haired Siamese, and a short-haired calico. The calico was a girl, but the other two cats were boys. The Francisco family wanted a girl cat. The Williams family wanted a boy cat, but they wanted one with short hair. Which cat did each family adopt? Fill in the table to solve the problem.

	Brown Tabby (short-haired boy)	Siamese (long-haired boy)	Calico (short-haired girl)
Francisco Family			
Landrum Family			
Williams Family			

_____

Name _____ Date _____

Unit 10 Review, page 2

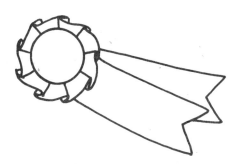

Show What You Know!

Solve each problem. Identify the strategy you used.

1. Lela, Zeb, and Remy won ribbons for running a race. The blue ribbon is for first place, the red ribbon is for second place, and the yellow ribbon is for third place. Lela did not come in first. Zeb came in just after Remy, but he beat Lela. Which ribbon did each runner win? Fill in the table to solve the problem.

	Blue Ribbon (1st place)	Red Ribbon (2nd place)	Yellow Ribbon (3rd place)
Lela			
Zeb			
Remy			

2. Tina traveled to see the Lincoln Memorial. The Lincoln Memorial is located in Washington, D.C. Is it **true** or **false** that Tina went to Washington, D.C.?

_____

3. On Thursday, Jarrod worked for 6 out of 8 hours because he was not feeling well. He only gets paid for the hours he works. He gets paid $10 an hour. Is it **true** or **false** that he earned $80 on Thursday?

_____

FLEX YOUR MATH MUSCLES

1

The Dolphins are playing the Whales in a swimming event. Points are scored each time a member crosses the finish line. The Dolphins are ahead 7 to 0. But not one man on the Dolphins has crossed the finish line. Can you explain this? Sure you can!

_____

_____

2

A man buys groceries at the supermarket and pays the cashier with a check. On it he writes a square inside a circle with 3 squiggly lines in it. The cashier looks at it and says: "I see you are a fireman." How can she tell? (HINT: The stuff on the check is only there to confuse you!)

_____

_____

3

Flex has a new hobby. He collects rocks. He went to the woods one day to find some new rocks. He had a bag of black rocks, a bag of white rocks, and a bag of green rocks. He neatly tagged each bag. Then it started to rain!

He ran back to his car, but the labels got mixed up. None of the bags had the right labels. Poor Flex. He had to look in all 3 bags and put back the right labels.

But there is an easier way. He could take 1 rock from 1 bag to see which rocks are in which bags. How can he do this? (HINT: All 3 bags have the wrong labels on them.)

_____

_____

Answer Key

NOTE: Students may use different strategies to solve problems on the unit reviews. The strategies listed are the most likely. Ask students to explain their strategies to ensure that they understand.

Assessment

Page 6
1. 355; 699; 81
2. 600; 225; 42
3. Saturday
4. 28 tickets

Page 7
5. ~~Joy's best friend scored 13 points on Friday.~~; 42 points
6. ~~It also has 9 sizes of dog and cat collars.~~; 15 puppies and kittens
7. 1,800 people
8. 100 students
9. 602 guppies
10. 85 fish

Page 8
11. $72 \div 9 = 8$ teams
12. $16 \times 8 = 128$ people
13. 12 cars
14. 1-2/8 or 1-1/4 ounces
15. 16 pounds
16. 20 years old

Page 9
17. $1.72
18. $15.60
19. 152 apples
20. $5.81
21. Answers may vary: pounds; yards.
22. Answers may vary: yards, gallons.
23. Ilda eats mushroom pizza.
24. Alex has red.

Working with Numbers

Page 11
1. 36
2. 224
3. 1,202

Page 12
1. 49; 95; 89; 559; 679
2. 61; 892; 418; 1,323; 1,190

Page 13
2. 6 ten thousands, 1 thousands, 0 hundreds, 2 tens, 3 ones
3. 8 millions, 9 hundred thousands, 2 ten thousands, 1 thousands, 8 hundreds, 0 tens, 0 ones
4. 6 hundred thousands, 4 ten thousands, 7 thousands, 3 hundreds, 6 tens, 9 ones
6. thousands
7. ones
8. ten thousands
10. 1 ones
11. 8 tens
12. 0 ten thousands

Page 14
1. striped flag; star flag; circle flag
2. 52
3. crayon
4. 123, 125

Page 15
2. fourteen thousand, one hundred ten
3. five thousand, two hundred eighty
4. eighty-six thousand, four hundred
5. three hundred forty-four
6. three hundred two
7. 1,000,000,000
8. 240
9. 89,000
10. Answers will vary.
11. Answers will vary.

Page 16
1. 156,823; 16,208,329
2. 8,067; 76,170; 741,038
3. 9,265,081; 1,972,493; 928,492
5. 3,081,056
6. 70,139

Page 17
1. ten thousands; Understand Place Value
2.

a.
T	O
1	4
+3	2
4	6

b.
H	T	O
	5	9
+	6	7
1	2	6

Make a Table
3. four thousand, one hundred, thirty-nine; Write Numbers in Words
4. 38, 41; Find a Pattern
5.
TH	H	T	O
1	4	5	6

Understand Place Value
6. 209, 053; Write Numbers in Digits

Page 18
1. See answer at end of Answer Key.
2.
a.
```
  519
+  87
-----
  606
```
b.
```
  836
+ 792
-----
 1628
```
Make a Table
3. ones; Understand Place Value
4.
TH	H	T	O
1	3	4	5

Understand Place Value, Use a Table

5. ○ △
Find a Pattern

Page 19
1. 7 thousands, 3 hundreds, 0 tens, 2 ones
2. $413 - 251 = 162$
3. 3,954; hundreds place value changes; 3 thousands, 6 hundreds, 5 tens, 4 ones
4. Answers may vary. 3,957; three thousand, nine hundred fifty-seven

Addition

Page 21
1. 56 pizzas
2. Saturday
3. pepperoni
4. $11.00
5. 1 pepperoni, 1 sausage OR 2 cheese, 1 pepperoni
6. $19.00

Page 22
1. ~~Each girl wore a red bathing suit~~; 32 children
2. ~~His team plays 20 games during a season~~; 9 games

Page 23
1. 70, 50, 120 cupcakes and cookies
2. 120, 100, 220 parents
3. 250, 370, 620 students; the second lunch period

Page 24
1. 6 kinds
2. 9 kinds; yes

Page 25
1. 4 ways
2. 9 ways

Page 26
1. Add; 674 students; Answers will vary.
2. Subtract; 275 pounds
3. Subtract; 42 cupcakes

Page 27
See table at end of Answer Key
1. 1,611
2. 1,210
3. chocolate chip
4. $1,874
5. $1,960

Page 28
1. 26 stamps; Identify Extra Information
2. About 100 miles; Use Estimation

3. 6 different combinations
   - Jules – Smokey
     Kitri – Banjo
   - Jules – Smokey
     Kitri – Ringo
   - Jules – Banjo
     Kitri – Smokey
   - Jules – Banjo
     Kitri – Ringo
   - Jules – Ringo
     Kitri – Smokey
   - Jules – Ringo
     Kitri – Banjo

   Make a List
4. add; 846 beads; Choose an Operation
5. add; 1,362 miles; Choose an Operation

Page 29
1. 4 boys; 5 girls; 24 children
2. 470 students
3. None (1 girl is a sister to all of the boys)

Subtraction

Page 30
3rd	4th	5th	total
49	39	61	149
14	57	55	126

1. 35 more 3rd graders
2. 43 more votes
3. Bo got more votes.
4. 100 votes
5. 23 more votes
6. Shay won.

Page 31
1. Subtract; 176 pages
2. Subtract; 43 minutes
3. Add; 348 pages

Page 32
1. ~~Mr. Garza drove 50 miles per hour all the way~~; 294 miles
2. 84 cards

Page 33
1. 1,700 miles
2. 1,400 fence posts
3. 1,600 head of cattle
4. 1,600 acres

Page 34
1. basketball
2. 20 votes
3. 240 students
4. 40 students

Page 35
1. 158 programs
2. 124 bags of peanuts

Page 35, continued
3. $2.00
4. Yes; $48 more
5. 28 pitches

Page 36
1. $3.00
2. 28 robins
3. 18 lbs
4. $123

Page 37
1. a. See answers at end of Answer Key.
1. b. 9
2. 13   3. 7
4. 2   5. 25
6. 21   7. 10

Page 38
1. subtract; $11; Choose an Operation
2. 28 cans of corn; Identify Extra Information
3. 4,200; Use Estimation
4. 167; Work Backward
5. 345 miles; Identify Substeps
6. cats; Use a Graph

Page 39
1. All months have 28 days.
2. Move one stick from the equals sign to the subtraction sign, so the problem reads:
   $|| = |||| - ||$

Multiplication
Page 40
1. 28×2; 56; yes
2. 54 hours; 14 hours

Page 41
1. 200-240; about 20 feet
2. No
3. 200 hours

Page 42
1. $554   2. pepperoni

Page 43
1. $336; Saturday; pepperoni
2. 2 tomatoes; 1 onion; 4 cups of cheese; Answers will vary.
3. $105

Page 44
1. Number jerseys: 20, 25, 30, 35, Tiffany's jersey is number 30.
2. 14, 17
3. 495, 594
4. 56, 59
5. 63, 70

Page 45
1. 42 golf balls
2. 155 pages

Page 46
1. 6 combinations

Page 47
1. multiply; 32 tomato plants; Choose an Operation
2. 32, 40; Find a Pattern
3. 7 radios; Work Backward
4. About 200; Use Estimation
5. 6 combinations
   • red paint – engine
     blue paint – passenger car
     green paint – caboose
   • red paint – engine
     green paint – passenger car
     blue paint – caboose
   • blue paint – engine
     red paint – passenger car
     green paint – caboose
   • blue paint – engine
     green paint – passenger car
     red paint – caboose
   • green paint – engine
     blue paint – passenger car
     red paint – caboose
   • green paint – engine
     red paint – passenger car
     blue paint – caboose
   Make a List

Page 48
See chart at end of Answer Key.
1. $192
2. $280
3. $160
4. $632
5. plain chocolates
6. chocolates with nuts

Page 49
1. 0
2. $0 + (9 \times 3) = 27$; Answers will vary.
3. 15 miles
4. 12 stamps

Division
Page 50
1. 5 watermelons
2. 6 sparklers

Page 51
1. 10 holds; Jeff knows the most.
2. 90 laps

Page 52
1. 4 free toppings
2. Sandra's number is 16.
3. $2

Page 53
Beware of the March Hare

Page 55
1. Monday: 15 chairs
   Tuesday: 10 chairs
   Wednesday: 6 chairs
   Thursday: 5 chairs
   Friday: 3 chairs
2. Monday

3. Friday
4. Monday
5. Friday

Page 56
1. $2.00
2. 50 necklaces
3. $6.00
4. 6 ribbons

Page 57
1. Thursday = 40 bags; Friday = 32 bags; Find a Pattern
2. $15 per hour; Work Backward, Choose an Operation, Practice Division
3. 3 packages; Choose an Operation
4. 12 dogs; Practice Division

Page 58
1. 24 books per shelf; The graph should be shaded accordingly. Make a Graph
2. 30 books per shelf; The graph should be shaded accordingly. Make a Graph
3. 28 books per shelf; The graph should be shaded accordingly. Make a Graph
4. The bookcase with 5 shelves. Use a Graph
5. 4 more books per shelf Use a Graph

Page 59
1. make applesauce
2. 3
3. Neither train is closer.

Mixed Operations
Page 61
1. 33 cans
2. 9 boxes
3. 72 biographies
4. 18 boxes
5. 6 calculators
6. 15 beakers
7. 25 pages
8. 6 microscopes

Page 62
1. 4 classes; 16 groups
2. 7 hot dogs; 2 packages

Page 63
1. $5.00
2. 789 jelly beans; Answers will vary.

Page 64
1. 31 animals
2. 18 horses; 31 sheep; 38 steers

Page 65
1. 6 feet
2. 3 cards

Page 66
1. 400 stars; Answers will vary.
2. 40 squares
3. 70 pages

Page 67
1. $20 \div 2 = 10$; 10 flowers in each row; Write a Number Sentence
2. About 14; Use Estimation
3. 20 laps; added; Choose an Operation
4. At least 18 pounds; Use Estimation
5. 6 guests were men; Guess and Check

Page 68
See chart at end of Answer Key.
1. 22
2. 14
3. 16
4. 20
5. 14
6. 18

Page 69
1. 8 people, 14 dogs
2. LAP
3. Fill the 5 gallon (small) bucket. Now pour the water from the small bucket into the 6 gallon (large) bucket. Again fill the small bucket. Fill the large bucket with 1 gallon from the small bucket. (Now you have 4 gallons in the small bucket.) Empty the large bucket. Pour the 4 gallons from the small bucket into the large 6 gallon bucket. Then fill the small 5 gallon bucket to measure exactly 9 gallons of water.
4. There's always a 1 in 2 (or 50%) chance of the penny landing heads up.

Fractions
Page 70
1. 3 parts, shade 1 section of Window B
2. 2 panes, 2/5
3. 3/6 or 1/2; 3/6 or 1/2

Page 71
1. 3 markers 2. 4 sheets
3. 4 jars   4. 6 people

Page 72
1. 1/4 because there are 4 people
2. 2/8 or 1/4
3. 2/6 or 1/3

Page 73
1. 6/17

Page 74
1. 83-4/5 miles; about 6,000 miles
2. 4-1/2 miles

Page 75
1. 1-2/4; Yes; 2/4 more
2. 4-2/12; No

Page 76
1. 6-11/12 feet
2. 1-1/12 feet; Answers will vary.

Page 77
1. 3 markers; Use Fractions
2. ;
Make a Drawing
3. Gregor put away 2/3. He still had 1/3 of his toys to put away.; Choose an Operation
4.

Define Fractions
5. 9-2/4 or 9-1/2 months; Add Mixed Numbers
6. 1-2/8 or 1-1/4 ounces; Subtract Mixed Numbers

Page 78
1.

Define Fractions
2. Evan has made 12/23 of the cards. He still needs to make 11/23 of the cards. Choose an Operation
3.

Make a Drawing
4. 21-11/16 inches; Add Mixed Numbers
5. 25 stars; Use Fractions
6. 28-15/20 or 28-3/4 pounds; Subtract Mixed Numbers

Page 79
1. 30 ÷ 1/2 = 60 + 10 = 70
2. Flex makes 2 laps every 4 minutes. In an hour, he makes 15 more laps than Pablo.
3. He started with $48.00
4. $25. The two mothers and two daughters were a grandmother, mother, and daughter.

Decimals and Money

Page 80
1. 10 dimes
2. 1/10
3. 4 quarters
4. 1/4
5. 10 nickels; 2 quarters
6. 1/2
7. 50¢
8. 41¢
9. $3.20
10. $0.07

Page 81
1. no; $1.02
2. $7.39

Page 82
1. $1.50; $2.00
2. $2.02
3. Shing spent more.

Page 83
1. $47.67
2. $180

Page 84
1. $50
2. $7.00
3. $18.45
4. 180 shirts

Page 85
1. $0.90; answers will vary
2. bagel, cookie; 10¢ or 20¢
3. banana
4. Answers will vary.

Page 86
1. missing fact: How much did Jenine's father give the clerk?
2. $1.25; extra fact: Candles are $2.00.

Page 87
1. 4; Change Money
2. $8.50; Add Money
3. $19.50; Multiply Money
4. 1/100; Change Money
5. $73.21; Divide Money
6. 1/4; Change Money

Page 88
1. This problem cannot be solved because I don't know much money Denise gave the cashier.; Identify Extra or Missing Information
2. The Hoovers bought 2 adults' tickets and 2 children's tickets. ; Guess and Check
3. 20 nickels; Change Money
4. $39.73; Subtract Money
5. 72 cents; Change Money, Add Money
6. $2.70; Identify Extra or Missing Information

Page 89
1. $5.00
2. $30; the second deal
3. the first job
4. 3

Measurement

Page 90
sample: yard; pound
1. See answer at end of Answer Key

Page 91
1. 400 cm   2. 2,100 cm

Page 92
1. 10 kg   2. 5 kg
3. 9,000 g   4. 3,000 g

Page 93
1. 500 mL   2. 1 L

Page 94
Answers may vary slightly.
1. cm, g   2. cm, mL
3. m, kg   4. cm, kg
5. m, kg   6. cm, g
7. cm, kg   8. g, mL
9. m, kg   10. g, mL
11. m, kg, L   12. m, kg
13. m, L   14. kg, L, m
15. m, kg   16. g, mL
17. cm, g   18. m, kg
19. m, L   20. cm, kg

Page 95
1. 0°C or less
2. 100°C or more
3. about 20°C
4. Answers will vary.
5. About 2–4° C
6. warm clothes; Answers will vary.
7. warm-weather activities; Answers will vary.
8. tropics or desert; Answers will vary.

Page 96
1. 2:45; 4:20; 9:05
2. clocks reading 3:05, 4:35, 10:00, 12:30, and 8:15
3. 1,440
4. 3,600
5. Answers will vary.

Page 97
1. 2,000 mL; Measure Liquids
2. Answers will vary but should indicate summer clothing (shorts, short sleeve shirt, bathing suit, etc.).; Measure Temperature
3.

Measure Time
4. 2 hours; Measure Time
5. length weight volume Work with Standard Units
6. 0° C; Measure Temperature

Page 98
1. cm, m; Choose a Measurement
2. miles; Work with Standard Units

3. 300 cm; Work with Metric Units
4. length weight volume Work with Standard Units
5. 3,000 g; Use Metric Weight
6. mL, L; Choose a Measurement

Page 99
1. 4:00 p.m.
2. 1.5 hours = 90 minutes; 1 hour 30 minutes = 90 minutes
3. 21 miles
4. 9 cups

Logic

Page 101
1. See answer at end of Answer Key.
2. See answer at end of Answer Key.
3. See answer at end of Answer Key.
4. See answer at end of Answer Key.

Page 103
1. See answer at end of Answer Key.
2. See answer at end of Answer Key.
3. See answer at end of Answer Key.

Page 104
1. See answer at end of Answer Key.
2. See answer at end of Answer Key.

Page 105
Adam could pat his own head and ask, "Did you do this?" Whatever the Yoo replied would mean "yes," and he'd know whether or not the Yoo was President.

Page 106
1. See answer at end of Answer Key.
2. See answer at end of Answer Key.

Page 107
1. See answer at end of Answer Key.
2. true; Identify True or False
3. false; Identify True or False

Page 108
1. All the swimmers are women.
2. He was wearing his uniform.
3. Since all the bags were labeled wrong, by taking 1 rock out, he can correct the label, and then switch the other two labels.

Answer Key
Problem Solving Strategies 4, SV 0515-4

Page 18

1.

	Hundred Millions	Ten Millions	Millions	Hundred Thousands	Ten Thousands	Thousands	Hundreds	Tens	Ones
a.	9	4	0	3	3	1	5	7	2
b.				1	0	2	3	8	5
c.						1	0	9	6

Understand Place Value; Use a Table

Page 27

Science Club Bake Sale

	Chocolate Chip Cookies	Peanut Butter Cookies	Sugar Cookies
Saturday	847	531	496
Sunday	764	679	517
Totals	1,611	1,210	1,013

Page 37

1. a.

	Blue	Green	White
Number of Cars on Lot	37	28	15
Number of Cars Sold	12	7	5

Page 48

	Plain Chocolates	Chocolates with Nuts	Chocolates with Fillings
Saturday Sales	64 boxes	56 boxes	40 boxes
Box of Plain Chocolates ($3 per box)	$192		
Box of Chocolates with Nuts ($5 per box)		$280	
Box of Chocolates with Fillings ($4 per box)			$160

Page 68

1.

	June	July	August	Totals
Mysteries	6	7	9	22
Science Fiction	6	5	3	14
Adventure	8	2	6	16
Totals	20	14	18	

Page 106

1. Esther's bracelet was blue.

	Blue Bracelet	Red Bracelet
Esther	YES	NO
Hector	NO	YES

Make a Table, Use Logical Reasoning

2.

	Brown Tabby (short-haired boy)	Siamese (long-haired boy)	Calico (short-haired girl)
Francisco Family			X
Landrum Family		X	
Williams Family	X		

Look for Clues, Make a Table, Use Logical Reasoning

Page 107

1.

	Blue Ribbon (1st place)	Red Ribbon (2nd place)	Yellow Ribbon (3rd place)
Lela			X
Zeb		X	
Remy	X		

Page 90

		Length	Weight	Volume
2.	candle	inches	ounce	not use
3.	thermos	inches	ounce	cup or pint
4.	truck	yard	ton	not use
5.	juice box	inches	ounce	cup

Page 101

1.

	pepperoni	cheese	
Linda	yes	no	
Julio	no	yes	

2.

	mystery	biography	riddles
Ryan	yes	no	no
Wanda	no	yes	no
Sai	no	no	yes

3.

	baseball	basketball	soccer
Angelo	yes	no	no
Wayne	no	yes	no
Adrienne	no	no	yes

4.

	$2	6 quarters	
Erica	yes	no	
James	no	yes	

Page 103

1.

	home	school	laptop
Kim	yes	no	no
Dee	no	yes	no
Paul	no	no	yes

2.

	river	rock	surfing
Steve	yes	no	no
Jesse	no	yes	no
Karim	no	no	yes

3.

	9:00	10:00	11:00
Kendra	no	yes	no
Nadia	yes	no	no
Brett	no	no	yes

Page 104

1.

	blonde	red	brown
Debbie	yes	no	no
Dave	no	no	yes
Donna	no	yes	no

2.

	principal	kindergarten	gym
Jackson	no	yes	no
Morales	no	no	yes
O'Hara	yes	no	no

Answer Key
Problem Solving Strategies 4, SV 0515-4